And now abide faith, hope, love,
these three;
but the greatest of these is love.
—

1 CORINTHIANS 13:13 NKJV

©2013 Freeman-Smith, a division of Worthy Media, Inc.
All rights reserved. No part of this publication may be reproduced, stored in a retrieval system, or transmitted in any form or by any means—electronic, mechanical, photocopy, recording, scanning, or other—except for brief quotations in critical reviews or articles, without the prior written permission of the publisher.
Freeman-Smith, a division of Worthy Media, Inc.
134 Franklin Road, Suite 200, Brentwood, Tennessee 37027

The quoted ideas expressed in this book (but not Scripture verses) are not, in all cases, exact quotations, as some have been edited for clarity and brevity. In all cases, the author has attempted to maintain the speaker's original intent. In some cases, quoted material for this book was obtained from secondary sources, primarily print media. While every effort was made to ensure the accuracy of these sources, the accuracy cannot be guaranteed. For additions, deletions, corrections, or clarifications in future editions of this text, please write Freeman-Smith.

The Holy Bible, King James Version

The Holy Bible, New King James Version (NKJV) Copyright © 1982 by Thomas Nelson, Inc. Used by permission.

New Century Version®. (NCV) Copyright © 1987, 1988, 1991 by Word Publishing, a division of Thomas Nelson, Inc. All rights reserved. Used by permission.

The Holman Christian Standard Bible™ (HCSB) Copyright © 1999, 2000, 2001 by Holman Bible Publishers. Used by permission.

The Holy Bible, New International Version®. (NIV) Copyright © 1973, 1978, 1984 International Bible Society. Used by permission of Zondervan. All rights reserved.

The Holy Bible. New Living Translation (NLT) copyright © 1996 Tyndale Charitable Trust. Used by permission of Tyndale House Publishers.

The New American Standard Bible®, (NASB) Copyright © 1960, 1962, 1963, 1968, 1971, 1972, 1973, 1975, 1977, 1995 by The Lockman Foundation. Used by permission.

Scripture taken from The Message. (MSG) Copyright © 1993, 1994, 1995, 1996, 2000, 2001, 2002. Used by permission of NavPress Publishing Group.

Cover Design by Kim Russell / Wahoo Designs
Page Layout by Bart Dawson

ISBN 978-1-60587-435-7

Printed in the United States of America

1 2 3 4 5—CHG—17 16 15 14 13

a WOMAN'S GARDEN of LOVE

TABLE OF CONTENTS

INTRODUCTION

The dictionary defines the word *garden* as "a plot of ground used for the cultivation of flowers, fruits, or vegetables." That definition is correct, as far as it goes. But those of us who regularly dig our hands into the soil know that a garden is much more than a place for growing plants. It is also a place to renew our spirits, to commune with God, and to marvel at the glory of His creation.

Love is like a garden: it can be cultivated or neglected. When you take the time and make the effort to cultivate lasting relationships, you will reap a cornucopia of blessings. This text is a collection of thirty heartwarming messages from God's Holy Word and from noted Christian thinkers. The ideas on these pages can help you build deeper, more meaningful relationships. And that's exactly what God wants for you and yours.

So, during the next thirty days, try this experiment: read one chapter a day and take the ideas in that chapter to heart. While you're at it, remember that your own faith in God, like a tender seedling, must be nurtured and protected. And, please remember that the most important seed you'll ever plant is the seed of Christ's love that you plant forever in your heart.

CHAPTER

1

A WOMAN'S GARDEN OF LOVE

We love Him because He first loved us.

—

1 JOHN 4:19 NKJV

Love, like young seedlings in a garden, must be cultivated with care. And love, like every other thing in our universe, begins with God.

God's love for you is deeper and more profound than you can fathom. And now, precisely because you are a wondrous creation treasured by God, a question presents itself: What will you do in response to God's love? Will you ignore it or embrace it? Will you return it or neglect it? The decision, of course, is yours and yours alone.

When you embrace God's love, you are forever changed. When you embrace God's love, you feel differently about yourself, your family, your friends, and your world. When you embrace God's love, you share His message and you obey His commandments.

When you accept the Father's grace and share His love, you are blessed here on earth and throughout all eternity. Accept His love today . . . and share it always.

A TIMELY TIP FROM THE GARDEN OF LOVE

Remember: God's love for you is too big to understand with your brain . . . but it's not too big to feel with your heart.

PROMISES FROM GOD'S WORD

For the Lord is good, and His love is eternal; His faithfulness endures through all generations.

PSALM 100:5 HCSB

A person's insight gives him patience, and his virtue is to overlook an offense.

PROVERBS 19:11 HCSB

[Because of] the Lord's faithful love we do not perish, for His mercies never end. They are new every morning; great is Your faithfulness!

LAMENTATIONS 3:22-23 HCSB

Help me, Lord my God; save me according to Your faithful love.

PSALM 109:26 HCSB

Whoever is wise will observe these things, and they will understand the lovingkindness of the Lord.

PSALM 107:43 NKJV

MORE GREAT IDEAS

Jesus loves us with fidelity, purity, constancy, and passion, no matter how imperfect we are.

STORMIE OMARTIAN

Snuggle in God's arms. When you are hurting, when you feel lonely or left out, let Him cradle you, comfort you, reassure you of His all-sufficient power and love.

KAY ARTHUR

There is no pit so deep that God's love is not deeper still.

CORRIE TEN BOOM

Being loved by Him whose opinion matters most gives us the security to risk loving, too—even loving ourselves.

GLORIA GAITHER

For God is, indeed, a wonderful Father who longs to pour out His mercy upon us, and whose majesty is so great that He can transform us from deep within.

ST. TERESA OF AVILA

Because his mercies are new every morning, you can find the courage to bring all of who you are to all of who he is.

SHEILA WALSH

The fact is, God no longer deals with us in judgment but in mercy. If people got what they deserved, this old planet would have ripped apart at the seams centuries ago. Praise God that because of His great love "we are not consumed, for his compassions never fail" (Lam. 3:22).

JONI EARECKSON TADA

God wants to reveal Himself as your heavenly Father. When you are hurting, you can run to Him and crawl up into His lap. When you wonder which way to turn, you can grasp His strong hand, and He'll guide you along life's path. When everything around you is falling apart, you'll feel your Father's arm around your shoulder to hold you together.

LISA WHELCHEL

With God, it's never "Plan B" or "second best." It's always "Plan A." And, if we let Him, He'll make something beautiful of our lives.

GLORIA GAITHER

God is a God of unconditional,
unremitting love,
a love that corrects and chastens
but never ceases.

—

KAY ARTHUR

A PRAYER FOR TODAY

Lord, I know that You love me. I will accept Your love—and share it—today and every day. Amen

୬୨ର

YOUR THOUGHTS ABOUT GOD'S LOVE

_____

_____

_____

_____

_____

_____

_____

_____

_____

_____

_____

_____

_____

_____

CHAPTER 2

THE GREATEST OF THESE . . .

Now these three remain: faith, hope, and love.
But the greatest of these is love.

—

1 CORINTHIANS 13:13 HCSB

As a woman, you know the profound love that you hold in your heart for your own family and friends. As a child of God, you can only imagine the infinite love that your Heavenly Father holds for you.

God made you in His own image and gave you salvation through the person of His Son Jesus Christ. And now, precisely because you are a wondrous creation treasured by God, a question presents itself: What will you do in response to the Creator's love? Will you ignore it or embrace it? Will you return it or neglect it? That decision, of course, is yours and yours alone.

When you embrace God's love, your life's purpose is forever changed. When you embrace God's love, you feel differently about yourself, your neighbors, your family, and your world. More importantly, you share God's message—and His love—with others.

Your Heavenly Father—a God of infinite love and mercy—is waiting to embrace you with open arms. Accept His love today and forever.

A TIMELY TIP FROM THE GARDEN OF LOVE

Be creative. There are many ways to say, "I love you." Find them. Use them. And keep using them.

PROMISES FROM GOD'S WORD

If I speak the languages of men and of angels, but do not have love, I am a sounding gong or a clanging cymbal.

1 CORINTHIANS 13:1 HCSB

Above all, keep your love for one another at full strength, since love covers a multitude of sins.

1 PETER 4:8 HCSB

I pray that you, being rooted and firmly established in love, may be able to comprehend with all the saints what is the breadth and width, height and depth, and to know the Messiah's love that surpasses knowledge, so you may be filled with all the fullness of God.

EPHESIANS 3:17-19 HCSB

Dear friends, if God loved us in this way, we also must love one another.

1 JOHN 4:11 HCSB

We love because He first loved us.

1 JOHN 4:19 HCSB

MORE GREAT IDEAS

Love is the seed of all hope. It is the enticement to trust, to risk, to try, and to go on.

GLORIA GAITHER

Love is not soft as water is; it is solid as a rock on which the waves of hatred beat in vain.

CORRIE TEN BOOM

Agape is a kind of love God demonstrates to one person through another.

BETH MOORE

Love is extravagant in the price it is willing to pay, the time it is willing to give, the hardships it is willing to endure, and the strength it is willing to spend. Love never thinks in terms of "how little," but always in terms of "how much." Love gives, love knows, and love lasts.

JONI EARECKSON TADA

Forgiveness is the precondition of love.

CATHERINE MARSHALL

Love alone makes heavy burdens light and bears in equal balance things pleasing and displeasing. Love bears a heavy burden and does not feel it, and love makes bitter things tasteful and sweet.

THOMAS À KEMPIS

Love always means sacrifice.

ELISABETH ELLIOT

Line by line, moment by moment, special times are etched into our memories in the permanent ink of everlasting love in our relationships.

GLORIA GAITHER

Homes that are built on anything other than love are bound to crumble.

BILLY GRAHAM

Our Lord does not care so much for the importance of our works as for the love with which they are done.

ST. TERESA OF AVILA

Prayer is the ultimate
love language.
It communicates in ways we can't.

—

STORMIE OMARTIAN

A PRAYER FOR TODAY

Dear God, let me share Your love with the world. Make me a woman of compassion. Help me to recognize the needs of others. Let me forgive those who have hurt me, just as You have forgiven me. And let the love of Your Son shine in me and through me today, tomorrow, and throughout all eternity. Amen

YOUR THOUGHTS ABOUT LOVE

CHAPTER

3

PRIORITIES
FOR THE JOURNEY

He said to them all, "If anyone desires to come after
Me, let him deny himself, and take up his cross
daily, and follow Me. For whoever desires to save
his life will lose it, but whoever loses his life
for My sake will save it."

—

LUKE 9:23-24 NKJV

"First things first." These words are easy to speak but hard to put into practice. For busy women living in a demanding world, placing first things first can be difficult indeed. Why? Because so many people are expecting so many things from us!

If you're having trouble prioritizing your day, perhaps you've been trying to organize your life according to your own plans, not God's. A better strategy, of course, is to take your daily obligations and place them in the hands of the One who created you. To do so, you must prioritize your day according to God's commandments, and you must seek His will and His wisdom in all matters. Then, you can face the day with the assurance that the same God who created our universe out of nothingness will help you place first things first in your own life.

Do you feel overwhelmed or confused? Turn the concerns of this day over to God—prayerfully, earnestly, and often. Then listen for His answer . . . and trust the answer He gives.

A TIMELY TIP FROM THE GARDEN OF LOVE

Unless you put first things first, you're bound to finish last. And don't forget that putting first things first means God first and family next.

PROMISES FROM GOD'S WORD

And I pray this: that your love will keep on growing in knowledge and every kind of discernment, so that you can determine what really matters and can be pure and blameless in the day of Christ.

PHILIPPIANS 1:9 HCSB

For where your treasure is, there your heart will be also.

LUKE 12:34 HCSB

Now it happened as they went that He entered a certain village; and a certain woman named Martha welcomed Him into her house. And she had a sister called Mary, who also sat at Jesus' feet and heard His word. But Martha was distracted with much serving, and she approached Him and said, "Lord, do You not care that my sister has left me to serve alone? Therefore tell her to help me." And Jesus answered and said to her, "Martha, Martha, you are worried and troubled about many things. But one thing is needed, and Mary has chosen that good part, which will not be taken away from her."

LUKE 10:38-42 NKJV

MORE GREAT IDEAS

His life is our light—our purpose and meaning and reason for living.

ANNE GRAHAM LOTZ

Sin is largely a matter of mistaken priorities. Any sin in us that is cherished, hidden, and not confessed will cut the nerve center of our faith.

CATHERINE MARSHALL

The manifold rewards of a serious, consistent prayer life demonstrate clearly that time with our Lord should be our first priority.

SHIRLEY DOBSON

The work of God is appointed. There is always enough time to do the will of God.

ELISABETH ELLIOT

It's incredible to realize that what we do each day has meaning in the big picture of God's plan.

BILL HYBELS

Great relief and satisfaction can come from seeking God's priorities for us in each season, discerning what is "best" in the midst of many noble opportunities, and pouring our most excellent energies into those things.

BETH MOORE

It's sobering to contemplate how much time, effort, sacrifice, compromise, and attention we give to acquiring and increasing our supply of something that is totally insignificant in eternity.

ANNE GRAHAM LOTZ

There were endless demands on Jesus' time. Still he was able to make that amazing claim of "completing the work you gave me to do." (John 17:4 NIV)

ELISABETH ELLIOT

We are most vulnerable to the piercing winds of doubt when we distance ourselves from the mission and fellowship to which Christ has called us.

JONI EARECKSON TADA

We set our eyes on the finish line, forgetting the past, and straining toward the mark of spiritual maturity and fruitfulness.

—

VONETTE BRIGHT

A PRAYER FOR TODAY

Dear Lord, today is a new day. Help me finish the important tasks first, even if those tasks are unpleasant. Don't let me put off until tomorrow what I should do today. Amen

YOUR THOUGHTS ABOUT PRIORITIES

_____

_____

_____

_____

_____

_____

_____

_____

_____

_____

_____

_____

_____

4

HE WANTS YOU TO SERVE

Worship the Lord your God and . . .
serve Him only.

—

MATTHEW 4:10 HCSB

We live in a world that glorifies power, prestige, fame, and money. But the words of Jesus teach us that the most esteemed men and women in this world are not the self-congratulatory leaders of society but are instead the humblest of servants.

Are you willing to become a humble servant for Christ? Are you willing to pitch in and make the world a better place, or are you determined to keep all your blessings to yourself? The answers to these questions will determine the quantity and the quality of the service you render to God and to His children.

Today, you may feel the temptation to take more than you give. You may be tempted to withhold your generosity. Or you may be tempted to build yourself up in the eyes of your friends. Resist those temptations. Instead, serve your friends quietly and without fanfare. Find a need and fill it . . . humbly. Lend a helping hand . . . anonymously. Share a word of kindness . . . with quiet sincerity. As you go about your daily activities, remember that the Savior of all humanity made Himself a servant, and we, as His followers, must do no less.

A TIMELY TIP FROM THE GARDEN OF LOVE

Jesus was a servant, and if you want to follow Him, you must be a servant, too—even when service requires sacrifice.

PROMISES FROM GOD'S WORD

If they serve Him obediently, they will end their days in prosperity and their years in happiness.

JOB 36:11 HCSB

If anyone serves Me, let him follow Me; and where I am, there My servant will be also. If anyone serves Me, him My Father will honor.

JOHN 12:26 NKJV

A person should consider us in this way: as servants of Christ and managers of God's mysteries. In this regard, it is expected of managers that each one be found faithful.

1 CORINTHIANS 4:1-2 HCSB

We must do the works of Him who sent Me while it is day. Night is coming when no one can work.

JOHN 9:4 HCSB

Serve the Lord with gladness.

PSALM 100:2 HCSB

MORE GREAT IDEAS

So many times we say that we can't serve God because we aren't whatever is needed. We're not talented enough or smart enough or whatever. But if you are in covenant with Jesus Christ, He is responsible for covering your weaknesses, for being your strength. He will give you His abilities for your disabilities!

KAY ARTHUR

In the very place where God has put us, whatever its limitations, whatever kind of work it may be, we may indeed serve the Lord Christ.

ELISABETH ELLIOT

God has lots of folks who intend to go to work for him "some day." What He needs is more people who are willing to work for Him today.

MARIE T. FREEMAN

Through our service to others, God wants to influence our world for Him.

VONETTE BRIGHT

God wants us to serve Him with a willing spirit, one that would choose no other way.

BETH MOORE

If you want to discover your spiritual gifts, start obeying God. As you serve Him, you will find that He has given you the gifts that are necessary to follow through in obedience.

ANNE GRAHAM LOTZ

Doing something positive toward another person is a practical approach to feeling good about yourself.

BARBARA JOHNSON

Our ultimate aim in life is not to be healthy, wealthy, prosperous, or problem free. Our ultimate aim in life is to bring glory to God.

ANNE GRAHAM LOTZ

I can usually sense that a leading is from the Holy Spirit when it calls me to humble myself, serve somebody, encourage somebody or give something away. Very rarely will the evil one lead us to do those kind of things.

BILL HYBELS

Jesus never asks us to give Him
what we don't have.
But He does demand that
we give Him all we do have
if we want to be a part of what
He wishes to do in the lives
of those around us!

—

ANNE GRAHAM LOTZ

A PRAYER FOR TODAY

Dear Lord, in weak moments, I seek to build myself up by placing myself ahead of others. But Your commandment, Father, is that I become a humble servant to those who need my encouragement, my help, and my love. Create in me a servant's heart. And, let me be a woman who follows in the footsteps of Your Son Jesus who taught us by example that to be great in Your eyes, Lord, is to serve others humbly, faithfully, and lovingly. Amen

೨೦

YOUR THOUGHTS ABOUT THE NEED TO SERVE

CHAPTER
5

THE JOYS OF FRIENDSHIP

Beloved, if God so loved us,
we also ought to love one another.

—

1 JOHN 4:11 NKJV

What is a friend? The dictionary defines the word *friend* as "a person who is attached to another by feelings of affection or personal regard." This definition is accurate, as far as it goes, but when we examine the deeper meaning of friendship, so many more descriptors come to mind: trustworthiness, loyalty, helpfulness, kindness, understanding, forgiveness, encouragement, humor, and cheerfulness, to mention but a few.

Genuine friendship should be treasured, protected, and nourished. And how do we do so? By observing the Golden Rule: As Christians, we are commanded to treat others as we wish to be treated (Matthew 7:12). When we treat others with kindness, courtesy, and respect, we build friendships that can last a lifetime. And God smiles.

Do you want to have trustworthy, encouraging friends? Then be one. And make no mistake: that's exactly the kind of friend that God wants you to be.

A TIMELY TIP FROM THE GARDEN OF LOVE

Remember that the friends you choose can make a profound impact on every other aspect of your life. So choose carefully and prayerfully.

PROMISES FROM GOD'S WORD

A friend loves at all times, and a brother is born for a difficult time.

PROVERBS 17:17 HCSB

Iron sharpens iron, and one man sharpens another.

PROVERBS 27:17 HCSB

Finally, all of you be of one mind, having compassion for one another; love as brothers, be tenderhearted, be courteous.

1 PETER 3:8 NKJV

The one who loves his brother remains in the light, and there is no cause for stumbling in him.

1 JOHN 2:10 HCSB

No one has greater love than this, that someone would lay down his life for his friends.

JOHN 15:13 HCSB

MORE GREAT IDEAS

Friendship is the greatest of worldly goods. Certainly to me it is the chief happiness of life. If I had to give a piece of advice to a young man about a place to live, I think I should say, "sacrifice almost everything to live where you can be near your friends." I know I am very fortunate in that respect.

C. S. LEWIS

We long to find someone who has been where we've been, who shares our fragile skies, who sees our sunsets with the same shades of blue.

BETH MOORE

Inasmuch as anyone pushes you nearer to God, he or she is your friend.

BARBARA JOHNSON

You could have been born in another time and another place, but God determined to "people" your life with these particular friends.

JONI EARECKSON TADA

The bond of human friendship has a sweetness of its own, binding many souls together as one.

ST. AUGUSTINE

Friends are like a quilt with lots of different shapes, sizes, colors, and patterns of fabric. But the end result brings you warmth and comfort in a support system that makes your life richer and fuller.

SUZANNE DALE EZELL

If you choose to awaken a passion for God, you will have to choose your friends wisely.

LISA BEVERE

The best times in life are made a thousand times better when shared with a dear friend.

LUCI SWINDOLL

What a great favor God does to those whom He places in the company of good people!

ST. TERESA OF AVILA

In friendship,
God opens your eyes
to the glories of Himself.

—

JONI EARECKSON TADA

A PRAYER FOR TODAY

Thank You, Lord, for the Friend I have in Jesus. And, thank You for the dear friends You have given me, the friends who enrich my life. I pray for them today, and ask Your blessings upon them. Amen

YOUR THOUGHTS ABOUT THE NEED TO SPEND QUIET TIME WITH GOD

CHAPTER

6

OPTIMISM NOW

Finally brothers, whatever is true, whatever is honorable, whatever is just, whatever is pure, whatever is lovely, whatever is commendable— if there is any moral excellence and if there is any praise—dwell on these things.

—

PHILIPPIANS 4:8 HCSB

Pessimism and Christianity don't mix. Why? Because Christians have every reason to be optimistic about life here on earth and life eternal. Mrs. Charles E. Cowman advised, "Never yield to gloomy anticipation. Place your hope and confidence in God. He has no record of failure."

Sometimes, despite our trust in God, we may fall into the spiritual traps of worry, frustration, anxiety, or sheer exhaustion, and our hearts become heavy. What's needed is plenty of rest, a large dose of perspective, and God's healing touch, but not necessarily in that order.

Today, make this promise to yourself and keep it: vow to be a hope-filled Christian. Think optimistically about your life, your profession, and your future. Trust your hopes, not your fears. Take time to celebrate God's glorious creation. And then, when you've filled your heart with hope and gladness, share your optimism with others. They'll be better for it, and so will you.

A TIMELY TIP FROM THE GARDEN OF LOVE

Be positive: If your thoughts tend toward the negative end of the spectrum, redirect them. How? You can start by counting your blessings and by thanking your Father in heaven. And while you're at it, train yourself to begin thinking thoughts that are more rational, more accepting, and more upbeat.

PROMISES FROM GOD'S WORD

My cup runs over. Surely goodness and mercy shall follow me all the days of my life; and I will dwell in the house of the Lord Forever.

PSALM 23:5-6 NKJV

Be strong and courageous, all you who put your hope in the LORD.

PSALM 31:24 HCSB

Make me hear joy and gladness.

PSALM 51:8 NKJV

But if we hope for what we do not see, we eagerly wait for it with patience.

ROMANS 8:25 HCSB

For God has not given us a spirit of fearfulness, but one of power, love, and sound judgment.

2 TIMOTHY 1:7 HCSB

MORE GREAT IDEAS

The Christian lifestyle is not one of legalistic do's and don'ts, but one that is positive, attractive, and joyful.

VONETTE BRIGHT

God surrounds you with opportunity. You and I are free in Jesus Christ, not to do whatever we want, but to be all that God wants us to be.

WARREN WIERSBE

Developing a positive attitude means working continually to find what is uplifting and encouraging.

BARBARA JOHNSON

We may run, walk, stumble, drive, or fly, but let us never lose sight of the reason for the journey, or miss a chance to see a rainbow on the way.

GLORIA GAITHER

Go forward confidently, energetically attacking problems, expecting favorable outcomes.

NORMAN VINCENT PEALE

Keep your feet on the ground, but let your heart soar as high as it will. Refuse to be average or to surrender to the chill of your spiritual environment.

A. W. TOZER

If you can't tell whether your glass is half-empty or half-full, you don't need another glass; what you need is better eyesight . . . and a more thankful heart.

MARIE T. FREEMAN

Don't miss the beautiful colors of the rainbow while you're looking for the pot of gold at the end of it!

BARBARA JOHNSON

Make the least of all that goes and the most of all that comes. Don't regret what is past. Cherish what you have. Look forward to all that is to come. And most important of all, rely moment by moment on Jesus Christ.

GIGI GRAHAM TCHIVIDJIAN

The people whom I have seen succeed best in life have always been cheerful and hopeful people who went about their business with a smile on their faces.

CHARLES KINGSLEY

It never hurts your eyesight
to look on
the bright side of things.

—

BARBARA JOHNSON

A PRAYER FOR TODAY

Dear Lord, I will look for the best in other people, I will expect the best from You, and I will try my best to do my best—today and every day. Amen

YOUR THOUGHTS ABOUT THE NEED TO BE OPTIMISTIC

_____

_____

_____

_____

_____

_____

_____

_____

_____

_____

_____

_____

CHAPTER

7

THE POWER OF
HIS PROMISES

Heaven and earth will pass away,
but My words will never pass away.
—

MATTHEW 24:35 HCSB

God's promises are found in a book like no other: the Holy Bible. The Bible is a roadmap for life here on earth and for life eternal. As Christians, we are called upon to trust its promises, to follow its commandments, and to share its Good News.

As believers, we must study the Bible each day and meditate upon its meaning for our lives. Otherwise, we deprive ourselves of a priceless gift from our Creator. God's Holy Word is, indeed, a transforming, life-changing, one-of-a-kind treasure. And, a passing acquaintance with the Good Book is insufficient for Christians who seek to obey God's Word and to understand His will.

God has made promises to mankind and to you. God's promises never fail and they never grow old. You must trust those promises and share them with your family, with your friends, and with the world.

A TIMELY TIP FROM THE GARDEN OF LOVE

Charles Swindoll writes, "There are four words I wish we would never forget, and they are, 'God keeps his word.'" And, when it comes to studying God's Word, school is always in session.

PROMISES FROM GOD'S WORD

All Scripture is inspired by God and is profitable for teaching, for rebuking, for correcting, for training in righteousness, so that the man of God may be complete, equipped for every good work.

2 TIMOTHY 3:16-17 HCSB

Every word of God is pure; He is a shield to those who put their trust in Him.

PROVERBS 30:5 NKJV

But the word of the Lord endures forever. And this is the word that was preached as the gospel to you.

1 PETER 1:25 HCSB

For the word of God is living and effective and sharper than any two-edged sword, penetrating as far as to divide soul, spirit, joints, and marrow; it is a judge of the ideas and thoughts of the heart.

HEBREWS 4:12 HCSB

The one who is from God listens to God's words. This is why you don't listen, because you are not from God.

JOHN 8:47 HCSB

MORE GREAT IDEAS

God's Word is a light not only to our path but also to our thinking. Place it in your heart today, and you will never walk in darkness.

JONI EARECKSON TADA

Words fail to express my love for this holy Book, my gratitude for its author, for His love and goodness. How shall I thank him for it?

LOTTIE MOON

Walking in faith brings you to the Word of God. There you will be healed, cleansed, fed, nurtured, equipped, and matured.

KAY ARTHUR

The Bible became a living book and a guide for my life.

VONETTE BRIGHT

God can see clearly no matter how dark or foggy the night is. Trust His Word to guide you safely home.

LISA WHELCHEL

I need the spiritual revival that comes from spending quiet time alone with Jesus in prayer and in thoughtful meditation on His Word.

ANNE GRAHAM LOTZ

Weave the unveiling fabric of God's word through your heart and mind. It will hold strong, even if the rest of life unravels.

GIGI GRAHAM TCHIVIDJIAN

Jesus is Victor. Calvary is the place of victory. Obedience is the pathway of victory. Bible study and prayer is the preparation for victory.

CORRIE TEN BOOM

Ignoring Him by neglecting prayer and Bible reading will cause you to doubt.

ANNE GRAHAM LOTZ

Daily Bible reading is essential to victorious living and real Christian growth.

BILLY GRAHAM

If we are not continually fed
with God's Word,
we will starve spiritually.

—

STORMIE OMARTIAN

A PRAYER FOR TODAY

Dear Lord, Your scripture is a light unto the world; let me study it, trust it, and share it with all who cross my path. In all that I do, help me be a woman who is a worthy witness for You as I share the Good News of Your perfect Son and Your perfect Word. Amen

❧

YOUR THOUGHTS ABOUT GOD'S WORD

_____

_____

_____

_____

_____

_____

_____

_____

_____

_____

_____

SENSING GOD'S PRESENCE

Draw near to God,
and He will draw near to you.

—

JAMES 4:8 HCSB

Since God is everywhere, we are free to sense His presence whenever we take the time to quiet our souls and turn our prayers to Him. But sometimes, amid the incessant demands of everyday life, we turn our thoughts far from God; when we do, we suffer.

Do you set aside quiet moments each day to offer praise to your Creator? As a woman who has received the gift of God's grace, you most certainly should. Silence is a gift that you give to yourself and to God. During these moments of stillness, you will often sense the infinite love and power of your Creator—and He, in turn, will speak directly to your heart.

The familiar words of Psalm 46:10 remind us to "Be still, and know that I am God." When we do so, we encounter the awesome presence of our loving Heavenly Father, and we are comforted in the knowledge that God is not just near. He is here.

A TIMELY TIP FROM THE GARDEN OF LOVE

If you're here, God is here. If you're there, God is, too. You can't get away from Him or His love . . . thank goodness!

PROMISES FROM GOD'S WORD

The Lord is near all who call out to Him, all who call out to Him with integrity. He fulfills the desires of those who fear Him; He hears their cry for help and saves them.

PSALM 145:18-19 HCSB

I have set the Lord always before me; because He is at my right hand I shall not be moved.

PSALM 16:8 NKJV

You will seek Me and find Me when you search for Me with all your heart.

JEREMIAH 29:13 HCSB

Surely goodness and mercy shall follow me all the days of my life: and I will dwell in the house of the Lord for ever.

PSALM 23:6 KJV

I am not alone, because the Father is with Me.

JOHN 16:32 HCSB

MORE GREAT IDEAS

If your heart has grown cold, it is because you have moved away from the fire of His presence.

BETH MOORE

Through the death and broken body of Jesus Christ on the Cross, you and I have been given access to the presence of God when we approach Him by faith in prayer.

ANNE GRAHAM LOTZ

It is God to whom and with whom we travel, and while He is the End of our journey, He is also at every stopping place.

ELISABETH ELLIOT

Give yourself a gift today: be present with yourself. God is. Enjoy your own personality. God does.

BARBARA JOHNSON

God is always near, but the more I prayed, the more this truth struck home.

ELIZABETH GEORGE

Oh! what a Savior, gracious to all, / Oh! how His blessings round us fall, / Gently to comfort, kindly to cheer, / Sleeping or waking, God is near.

FANNY CROSBY

The next time you hear a baby laugh or see an ocean wave, take note. Pause and listen as his Majesty whispers ever so gently, "I'm here."

MAX LUCADO

If you want to hear God's voice clearly and you are uncertain, then remain in His presence until He changes that uncertainty. Often, much can happen during this waiting for the Lord. Sometimes, he changes pride into humility, doubt into faith and peace.

CORRIE TEN BOOM

Our souls were made to live in an upper atmosphere, and we stifle and choke if we live on any lower level. Our eyes were made to look off from these heavenly heights, and our vision is distorted by any lower gazing.

HANNAH WHITALL SMITH

As I wander from village to village,
I feel it is no idle fancy that
the Master walks beside me and
I hear his voice saying gently,
"I am with you always,
even unto the end."

—

LOTTIE MOON

A PRAYER FOR TODAY

Dear Lord, You are always with me. Thank You for never leaving my side, even for a moment! Amen

৩ৡৡ

YOUR THOUGHTS ABOUT GOD'S PRESENCE

_____

_____

_____

_____

_____

_____

_____

_____

_____

_____

_____

_____

_____

_____

CHAPTER

9

FORGIVENESS NOW

And whenever you stand praying,
if you have anything against anyone, forgive him,
so that your Father in heaven may also
forgive you your wrongdoing.

—

MARK 11:25 HCSB

Even the most mild-mannered women will, on occasion, have reason to become angry with the inevitable shortcomings of family members and friends. But wise women are quick to forgive others, just as God has forgiven them.

The commandment to forgive others is clearly a part of God's Word, but oh how difficult a commandment it can be to follow. Because we are imperfect beings, we are quick to anger, quick to blame, slow to forgive, and even slower to forget. No matter. Even when forgiveness is difficult, God's instructions are straightforward: As Christians who have received the gift of forgiveness, we must now share that gift with others.

If, in your heart, you hold bitterness against even a single person, forgive. If there exists even one person, alive or dead, whom you have not forgiven, follow God's commandment and His will for your life: forgive. If you are embittered against yourself for some past mistake or shortcoming, forgive. Then, to the best of your abilities, forget, and move on. Bitterness and regret are not part of God's plan for your life. Forgiveness is. And once you've forgiven others, you can then turn your thoughts to a far more pleasant subject: the incredibly bright future that God has promised.

PROMISES FROM GOD'S WORD

All bitterness, anger and wrath, insult and slander must be removed from you, along with all wickedness. And be kind and compassionate to one another, forgiving one another, just as God also forgave you in Christ.

EPHESIANS 4:31-32 HCSB

A person's insight gives him patience, and his virtue is to overlook an offense.

PROVERBS 19:11 HCSB

Then Peter came to Him and said, "Lord, how many times could my brother sin against me and I forgive him? As many as seven times?" "I tell you, not as many as seven," Jesus said to him, "but 70 times seven."

MATTHEW 18:21-22 HCSB

A TIMELY TIP FROM THE GARDEN OF LOVE

Forgiveness is its own reward. Bitterness is its own punishment. Guard your words and your thoughts accordingly.

MORE GREAT IDEAS

Forgiveness is the key that unlocks the door of resentment and the handcuffs of hate. It is a power that breaks the chains of bitterness and the shackles of selfishness.

CORRIE TEN BOOM

How often should you forgive the other person? Only as many times as you want God to forgive you!

MARIE T. FREEMAN

Sometimes, we need a housecleaning of the heart.

CATHERINE MARSHALL

To be a Christian means to forgive the inexcusable, because God has forgiven the inexcusable in you.

C. S. LEWIS

I believe that forgiveness can become a continuing cycle: because God forgives us, we're to forgive others; because we forgive others, God forgives us. Scripture presents both parts of the cycle.

SHIRLEY DOBSON

Forgiveness is actually the best revenge because it not only sets us free from the person we forgive, but it frees us to move into all that God has in store for us.

STORMIE OMARTIAN

Forgiveness is contagious. First you forgive them, and pretty soon, they'll forgive you, too.

MARIE T. FREEMAN

Jesus had a forgiving and understanding heart. If he lives within us, mercy will temper our relationships with our fellow men.

BILLY GRAHAM

There is no use in talking as if forgiveness were easy. I could say of a certain man, "Have I forgiven him more times than I can count?" For we find that the work of forgiveness has to be done over and over again.

C. S. LEWIS

God expects us to forgive others as He has forgiven us; we are to follow His example by having a forgiving heart.

VONETTE BRIGHT

It is better to forgive and forget
than to resent and remember.

—

BARBARA JOHNSON

A PRAYER FOR TODAY

Dear Lord, let forgiveness rule my heart, even when forgiveness is difficult. Let me be Your obedient servant, Lord, and let me be a woman who forgives others just as You have forgiven me. Amen

ൟ

YOUR THOUGHTS ABOUT FORGIVENESS

_____

_____

_____

_____

_____

_____

_____

_____

_____

_____

_____

_____

_____

CHAPTER

10

FINDING PURPOSE

*For it is God who is working among you
both the willing and the working
for His good purpose.*

—

PHILIPPIANS 2:13 HCSB

"**W**hat on earth does God intend for me to do with my life?" It's an easy question to ask but, for many of us, a difficult question to answer. Why? Because God's purposes aren't always clear to us. Sometimes we wander aimlessly in a wilderness of our own making. And sometimes, we struggle mightily against God in an unsuccessful attempt to find success and happiness through our own means, not His.

If you're a woman who sincerely seeks God's guidance, He will give it. But, He will make His revelations known to you in a way and in a time of His choosing, not yours, so be patient. If you prayerfully petition God and work diligently to discern His intentions, He will, in time, lead you to a place of joyful abundance and eternal peace.

Sometimes, God's intentions will be clear to you; other times, God's plan will seem uncertain at best. But even on those difficult days when you are unsure which way to turn, you must never lose sight of these overriding facts: God created you for a reason; He has important work for you to do; and He's waiting patiently for you to do it.

A TIMELY TIP FROM THE GARDEN OF LOVE

God has a wonderful plan for your life. And the time to start looking for that plan—and living it—is now. (Psalm 16:11)

PROMISES FROM GOD'S WORD

I will instruct you and show you the way to go; with My eye on you, I will give counsel.

PSALM 32:8 HCSB

To everything there is a season, a time for every purpose under heaven.

ECCLESIASTES 3:1 NKJV

We know that all things work together for the good of those who love God: those who are called according to His purpose.

ROMANS 8:28 HCSB

You reveal the path of life to me; in Your presence is abundant joy; in Your right hand are eternal pleasures.

PSALM 16:11 HCSB

Commit your activities to the Lord and your plans will be achieved.

PROVERBS 16:3 HCSB

MORE GREAT IDEAS

There is something about having endured great loss that brings purity of purpose and strength of character.

BARBARA JOHNSON

Only God's chosen task for you will ultimately satisfy. Do not wait until it is too late to realize the privilege of serving Him in His chosen position for you.

BETH MOORE

Great relief and satisfaction can come from seeking God's priorities for us in each season, discerning what is "best" in the midst of many noble opportunities, and pouring our most excellent energies into those things.

BETH MOORE

How much of our lives are, well, so daily. How often our hours are filled with the mundane, seemingly unimportant things that have to be done, whether at home or work. These very "daily" tasks could become a celebration of praise. "It is through consecration," someone has said, "that drudgery is made divine."

GIGI GRAHAM TCHIVIDJIAN

His life is our light—our purpose and meaning and reason for living.

ANNE GRAHAM LOTZ

In the very place where God has put us, whatever its limitations, whatever kind of work it may be, we may indeed serve the Lord Christ.

ELISABETH ELLIOT

God specializes in things fresh and firsthand. His plans for you this year may outshine those of the past. He's prepared to fill your days with reasons to give Him praise.

JONI EARECKSON TADA

Whether you have twenty years left, ten years, one year, one month, one day, or just one hour, there is something very important God wants you to do that can add to His kingdom and your blessing.

BILL BRIGHT

The Christian life is not simply following principles but being empowered to fulfill our purpose: knowing and exalting Christ.

FRANKLIN GRAHAM

If you want purpose and meaning
and satisfaction and fulfillment
and peace and hope and joy and
abundant life that lasts forever,
look to Jesus.

—

ANNE GRAHAM LOTZ

A PRAYER FOR TODAY

Lord, You've got something You want me to do—help me to figure out exactly what it is. Give me Your blessings and lead me along a path that is pleasing to You . . . today, tomorrow, and forever. Amen

⅋

YOUR THOUGHTS ABOUT YOUR PURPOSE

_____

_____

_____

_____

_____

_____

_____

_____

_____

_____

_____

_____

THE POWER OF PATIENCE

Rejoice in hope; be patient in affliction;
be persistent in prayer.

—

ROMANS 12:12 HCSB

Psalm 37:7 commands us to wait patiently for God. But as busy women in a fast-paced world, many of us find that waiting quietly for God is difficult. Why? Because we are fallible human beings seeking to live according to our own timetables, not God's. In our better moments, we realize that patience is not only a virtue, but it is also a commandment from God.

We human beings are impatient by nature. We know what we want, and we know exactly when we want it: NOW! But, God knows better. He has created a world that unfolds according to His plans, not our own. As believers, we must trust His wisdom and His goodness.

God instructs us to be patient in all things. We must be patient with our families, our friends, and our associates. We must also be patient with our Creator as He unfolds His plan for our lives. And that's as it should be. After all, think of how patient God has been with us.

A TIMELY TIP FROM THE GARDEN OF LOVE

God asks you to be a positive example to your family, to your friends, and to the world. The rest is up to you.

PROMISES FROM GOD'S WORD

A patient spirit is better than a proud spirit.

ECCLESIASTES 7:8 HCSB

My brethren, count it all joy when you fall into various trials, knowing that the testing of your faith produces patience. But let patience have its perfect work, that you may be perfect and complete, lacking nothing.

JAMES 1:2-4 NKJV

Love is patient; love is kind.

1 CORINTHIANS 13:4 HCSB

Therefore the Lord is waiting to show you mercy, and is rising up to show you compassion, for the Lord is a just God. Happy are all who wait patiently for Him.

ISAIAH 30:18 HCSB

Be gentle to everyone, able to teach, and patient.

2 TIMOTHY 2:23 HCSB

MORE GREAT IDEAS

Waiting is an essential part of spiritual discipline. It can be the ultimate test of faith.

ANNE GRAHAM LOTZ

We must learn to wait. There is grace supplied to the one who waits.

MRS. CHARLES E. COWMAN

Those who have had to wait and work for happiness seem to enjoy it more, because they never take it for granted.

BARBARA JOHNSON

In the Bible, patience is not a passive acceptance of circumstances. It is a courageous perseverance in the face of suffering and difficulty.

WARREN WIERSBE

Let me encourage you to continue to wait with faith. God may not perform a miracle, but He is trustworthy to touch you and make you whole where there used to be a hole.

LISA WHELCHEL

When we read of the great Biblical leaders, we see that it was not uncommon for God to ask them to wait, not just a day or two, but for years, until God was ready for them to act.

GLORIA GAITHER

If you want to hear God's voice clearly and you are uncertain, then remain in His presence until He changes that uncertainty. Often much can happen during this waiting for the Lord. Sometimes he changes pride into humility; doubt into faith and peace.

CORRIE TEN BOOM

The next time you're disappointed, don't panic. Don't give up. Just be patient and let God remind you he's still in control.

MAX LUCADO

If God is diligent, surely we ought to be diligent in doing our duty to Him. Think how patient and diligent God has been to us!

OSWALD CHAMBERS

Waiting is the hardest
kind of work, but God knows best,
and we may joyfully leave
all in His hands.

—

LOTTIE MOON

A PRAYER FOR TODAY

Lord, give me patience. When I am hurried, give me peace. When I am frustrated, give me perspective. When I am angry, let me turn my heart to You. Today, let me become a more patient woman, Dear Lord, as I trust in You and in Your master plan for my life. Amen

❦

YOUR THOUGHTS ABOUT WAYS
TO BE MORE PATIENT

12

THE RULE THAT'S GOLDEN

Therefore, whatever you want others to do for you,
do also the same for them—
this is the Law and the Prophets.

—

MATTHEW 7:12 HCSB

The words of Matthew 7:12 remind us that, as believers in Christ, we are commanded to treat others as we wish to be treated. This commandment is, indeed, the Golden Rule for Christians of every generation.

Kindness is a choice. Sometimes, when we feel happy or prosperous, we find it easy to be kind. Other times, when we are discouraged or tired, we can scarcely summon the energy to utter a single kind word. But, God's commandment is clear: we must observe the Golden Rule "in everything." God intends that we make the conscious choice to treat others with kindness and respect, no matter our circumstances, no matter our emotions. Kindness, therefore, is a choice that we, as Christians must make many times each day.

When we weave the thread of kindness into the very fabric of our lives, we give a priceless gift to others, and we give glory to the One who gave His life for us. As believers, we must do no less.

A TIMELY TIP FROM THE GARDEN OF LOVE

Remember this: when you treat others with respect, you won't just feel better about them, you'll feel better about yourself, too.

PROMISES FROM GOD'S WORD

Just as you want others to do for you, do the same for them.

LUKE 6:31 HCSB

See that no one renders evil for evil to anyone, but always pursue what is good both for yourselves and for all.

1 THESSALONIANS 5:15 NKJV

If you really carry out the royal law prescribed in Scripture, You shall love your neighbor as yourself, you are doing well.

JAMES 2:8 HCSB

And let us not grow weary while doing good, for in due season we shall reap if we do not lose heart.

GALATIANS 6:9 NKJV

For we are His workmanship, created in Christ Jesus for good works, which God prepared beforehand that we should walk in them.

EPHESIANS 2:10 NKJV

MORE GREAT IDEAS

Our lives, we are told, are but fleeting at best, / Like roses they fade and decay; / Then let us do good while the present is ours, / Be useful as long as we stay.

FANNY CROSBY

Before you can dry another's tears, you too must weep.

BARBARA JOHNSON

Do all the good you can. By all the means you can. In all the ways you can. In all the places you can. At all the times you can. To all the people you can. As long as ever you can.

JOHN WESLEY

The Golden Rule starts at home, but it should never stop there.

MARIE T. FREEMAN

There is but one good; that is God. Everything else is good when it looks to Him and bad when it turns from Him.

C. S. LEWIS

Faith never asks whether good works are to be done, but has done them before there is time to ask the question, and it is always doing them.

MARTIN LUTHER

It is one of the most beautiful compensations of life that no one can sincerely try to help another without helping herself.

BARBARA JOHNSON

God does not want us to work for Him, nor does He want to be our helper. Rather, He wants to do His work in and through us.

VONETTE BRIGHT

All kindness and good deeds, we must keep silent. The result will be an inner reservoir of personality power.

CATHERINE MARSHALL

Let no one ever come to you without leaving better and happier. Be the living expression of God's kindness: kindness in your face, kindness in your eyes, kindness in your smile.

MOTHER TERESA

Kindness in this world will do
much to help others,
not only to come into the light,
but also to grow in grace
day by day.

—

FANNY CROSBY

A PRAYER FOR TODAY

Dear Lord, because I expect kindness from others, let me be kind. Because I wish to be loved, let me be loving. Because I need forgiveness, let me be merciful. In all things, Lord, let me live by the Golden Rule that is the commandment of Your Son Jesus. Amen

YOUR THOUGHTS ABOUT THE REWARDS OF KINDNESS

_____

_____

_____

_____

_____

_____

_____

_____

_____

_____

_____

FINDING STRENGTH

And He said to me,
"My grace is sufficient for you,
for My strength is made perfect in weakness."

—

2 CORINTHIANS 12:9 NKJV

Where do you go to find strength? The gym? The health food store? The espresso bar? There's a better source of strength, of course, and that source is God. He is a never-ending source of strength and courage if you call upon Him.

Are you an energized Christian? You should be. But if you're not, you must seek strength and renewal from the source that will never fail: that source, of course, is your Heavenly Father. And rest assured—when you sincerely petition Him, He will give you all the strength you need to live victoriously for Him.

Have you "tapped in" to the power of God? Have you turned your life and your heart over to Him, or are you muddling along under your own power? The answer to this question will determine the quality of your life here on earth and the destiny of your life throughout all eternity. So start tapping in—and remember that when it comes to strength, God is the Ultimate Source.

A TIMELY TIP FROM THE GARDEN OF LOVE

Feeling exhausted? Try this: Start getting more sleep each night; begin a program of regular, sensible exercise; avoid harmful food and drink; and turn your problems over to God . . . and the greatest of these is "turn your problems over to God."

PROMISES FROM GOD'S WORD

The Lord is my strength and my song; He has become my salvation.

EXODUS 15:2 HCSB

Finally, be strengthened by the Lord and by His vast strength.

EPHESIANS 6:10 HCSB

You, therefore, my child, be strong in the grace that is in Christ Jesus.

2 TIMOTHY 2:1 HCSB

He gives strength to the weary and strengthens the powerless.

ISAIAH 40:29 HCSB

But those who wait on the Lord shall renew their strength; they shall mount up with wings like eagles, they shall run and not be weary, they shall walk and not faint.

ISAIAH 40:31 NKJV

MORE GREAT IDEAS

When you and I are related to Jesus Christ, our strength and wisdom and peace and joy and love and hope may run out, but His life rushes in to keep us filled to the brim. We are showered with blessings, not because of anything we have or have not done, but simply because of Him.

ANNE GRAHAM LOTZ

Victory is the result of Christ's life lived out in the believer. It is important to see that victory, not defeat, is God's purpose for His children.

CORRIE TEN BOOM

We are never stronger than the moment we admit we are weak.

BETH MOORE

God does not dispense strength and encouragement like a druggist fills your prescription. The Lord doesn't promise to give us something to take so we can handle our weary moments. He promises us Himself. That is all. And that is enough.

CHARLES SWINDOLL

When the dream of our heart is one that God has planted there, a strange happiness flows into us. At that moment, all of the spiritual resources of the universe are released to help us. Our praying is then at one with the will of God and becomes a channel for the Creator's purposes for us and our world.

CATHERINE MARSHALL

Sometimes I think spiritual and physical strength is like manna: you get just what you need for the day, no more.

SUZANNE DALE EZELL

One reason so much American Christianity is a mile wide and an inch deep is that Christians are simply tired. Sometimes you need to kick back and rest for Jesus' sake.

DENNIS SWANBERG

Hope can give us life. It can provide energy that would otherwise do us in completely if we tried to operate in our own strength.

BARBARA JOHNSON

Worry does not empty
tomorrow of its sorrow;
it empties today of its strength.

—

CORRIE TEN BOOM

A PRAYER FOR TODAY

Dear Heavenly Father, You are my strength and my protector. When I am troubled, You comfort me. When I am discouraged, You lift me up. When I am afraid, You deliver me. Let me turn to You, Lord, when I am weak. In times of adversity, let me trust Your plan, Lord, and whatever my circumstances, let me look to You for my strength and my salvation. Amen

YOUR THOUGHTS ABOUT FINDING STRENGTH

THE IMPORTANCE OF CHARACTER

As in water face reflects face,
so a man's heart reveals the man.

—

PROVERBS 27:19 NKJV

Honesty is the best policy, but it is not always the easiest policy. Sometimes, the truth hurts, and sometimes, it's tough to be a person of integrity . . . tough, but essential.

Billy Graham observed, "Integrity is the glue that holds our way of life together. We must constantly strive to keep our integrity intact. When wealth is lost, nothing is lost; when health is lost, something is lost; when character is lost, all is lost." Loyal friends agree.

Integrity is built slowly over a lifetime. It is the sum of every right decision and every honest word. It is forged on the anvil of honorable work and polished by the twin virtues of honesty and fairness. Integrity is a precious thing—difficult to build but easy to tear down. As believers in Christ, we must seek to live each day with discipline, honesty, and faith. When we do, integrity becomes a habit. And God smiles.

A TIMELY TIP FROM THE GARDEN OF LOVE

Character matters. Your ability to witness for Christ depends more upon your actions than your words.

PROMISES FROM GOD'S WORD

As the water reflects the face, so the heart reflects the person.

PROVERBS 27:19 HCSB

Do not be deceived: "Evil company corrupts good habits."

1 CORINTHIANS 15:33 NKJV

We also rejoice in our afflictions, because we know that affliction produces endurance, endurance produces proven character, and proven character produces hope.

ROMANS 5:3-4 HCSB

Now don't be afraid, my daughter. I will do for you whatever you say, since all the people in my town know that you are a woman of noble character.

RUTH 3:11 HCSB

A good name is to be chosen rather than great riches, loving favor rather than silver and gold.

PROVERBS 22:1 NKJV

MORE GREAT IDEAS

Character is not something highly valued in this society, so it is most important that the development of strong character be emphasized and rewarded in the home.

CHARLES STANLEY

There is no way to grow a saint overnight. Character, like the oak tree, does not spring up like a mushroom.

VANCE HAVNER

God never called us to naïveté. He called us to integrity. The biblical concept of integrity emphasizes mature innocence not childlike ignorance.

BETH MOORE

Character is both developed and revealed by tests, and all of life is a test.

RICK WARREN

Character is made in the small moments of our lives.

PHILLIPS BROOKS

Much guilt arises in the life of the believer from practicing the chameleon life of environmental adaptation.

BETH MOORE

Integrity is not a given factor in everyone's life. It is a result of self-discipline, inner trust, and a decision to be relentlessly honest in all situations in our lives.

JOHN MAXWELL

Honesty has a beautiful and refreshing simplicity about it. No ulterior motives. No hidden meanings. As honesty and integrity characterize our lives, there will be no need to manipulate others.

CHARLES SWINDOLL

The trials of life can be God's tools for engraving His image on our character.

WARREN WIERSBE

There's nothing like the power of integrity. It is a characteristic so radiant, so steady, so consistent, so beautiful, that it makes a permanent picture in our minds.

FRANKLIN GRAHAM

The single most important element
in any human relationship
is honesty—with oneself,
with God, and with others.

—

CATHERINE MARSHALL

A PRAYER FOR TODAY

Dear Lord, make me a woman whose conduct is honorable. Make me a friend whose words are true. Give me the wisdom to know right from wrong, and give me the courage—and the skill—to do what needs to be done in the service of Your Son. Amen

YOUR THOUGHTS ABOUT THE IMPORTANCE OF INTEGRITY

CHAPTER

15

BELIEVE IN YOURSELF!

*For You have made him a little lower
than the angels, and You have crowned him
with glory and honor.*

—

PSALM 8:5 NKJV

Do you believe that you deserve the best, and that you can achieve the best? Or have you convinced yourself that you're a second-tier talent who'll be lucky to finish far back in the pack? Before you answer that question, remember this: God sent His Son so that you might enjoy the abundant life that Jesus describes in the familiar words of John 10:10. But, God's gifts are not guaranteed—it's up to you to claim them.

As you plan for the next stage of your life's journey, promise yourself that when it comes to the important things in life, you won't settle for second best. And what, pray tell, are the "important things"? Your faith, your family, your health, and your relationships, for starters.

So if you want to achieve the best that life has to offer, convince yourself that you have the ability to earn the rewards you desire. Become sold on yourself—sold on your opportunities, sold on your potential, sold on your abilities. If you're sold on yourself, chances are the world will soon become sold too, and the results will be beautiful.

A TIMELY TIP FROM THE GARDEN OF LOVE

Don't worry too much about self-esteem. Instead, worry more about living a life that is pleasing to God. Learn to think optimistically. Find a worthy purpose. Find people to love and people to serve. When you do, your self-esteem will, on most days, take care of itself.

PROMISES FROM GOD'S WORD

How happy are those whose way is blameless, who live according to the law of the Lord! Happy are those who keep His decrees and seek Him with all their heart.

PSALM 119:1-2 HCSB

Finally, brethren, whatever things are true, whatever things are noble, whatever things are just, whatever things are pure, whatever things are lovely, whatever things are of good report, if there is any virtue and if there is anything praiseworthy— meditate on these things.

PHILIPPIANS 4:8 NKJV

Happy is the one whose help is the God of Jacob, whose hope is in the Lord his God.

PSALM 146:5 HCSB

Trust in the Lord with all your heart, and lean not on your own understanding; in all your ways acknowledge Him, and He shall direct your paths.

PROVERBS 3:5-6 NKJV

If God is for us, who is against us?

ROMANS 8:31 HCSB

MORE GREAT IDEAS

The Creator has made us each one of a kind. There is nobody else exactly like us, and there never will be. Each of us is his special creation and is alive for a distinctive purpose.

LUCI SWINDOLL

When it comes to our position before God, we're perfect. When he sees each of us, he sees one who has been made perfect through the One who is perfect—Jesus Christ.

MAX LUCADO

God often reveals His direction for our lives through the way He made us: with a certain personality and unique skills.

BILL HYBELS

Give yourself a gift today: be present with yourself. God is. Enjoy your own personality. God does.

BARBARA JOHNSON

Your self worth is more important than your net worth.

ANONYMOUS

Instead of being frustrated and overwhelmed by all that is going on in our world, go to the Lord and ask Him to give you His eternal perspective.

KAY ARTHUR

Mature people are not emotionally and spiritually devastated by every mistake they make. They are able to maintain some kind of balance in their lives.

JOYCE MEYER

Comparison is the root of all feelings of inferiority.

JAMES DOBSON

I was learning something important: we are most vulnerable to the piercing winds of doubt when we distance ourselves from the mission and fellowship to which Christ has called us. Our night of discouragement will seem endless and our task impossible, unless we recognize that He stands in our midst.

JONI EARECKSON TADA

Being loved by Him whose opinion matters most gives us the security to risk loving, too— even loving ourselves.

—

GLORIA GAITHER

A PRAYER FOR TODAY

Dear Lord, thank You for Your Son. Because Jesus loves me, I will feel good about myself, my family, and my future. Amen

༄

YOUR THOUGHTS ABOUT WAYS TO MAINTAIN A HEALTHY SELF-ESTEEM

_____

_____

_____

_____

_____

_____

_____

_____

_____

_____

_____

_____

16

TRUST HIM

Trust in the Lord with all your heart,
and do not rely on your own understanding;
think about Him in all your ways,
and He will guide you on the right paths.

—

PROVERBS 3:5-6 HCSB

When our dreams come true and our plans prove successful, we find it easy to thank our Creator and easy to trust His divine providence. But in times of sorrow or hardship, we may find ourselves questioning God's plans for our lives.

On occasion, you will confront circumstances that trouble you to the very core of your soul. It is during these difficult days that you must find the wisdom and the courage to trust your Heavenly Father despite your circumstances.

Are you a woman who seeks God's blessings for yourself and your family? Then trust Him. Trust Him with your relationships. Trust Him with your priorities. Follow His commandments and pray for His guidance. Trust Your Heavenly Father day by day, moment by moment—in good times and in trying times. Then, wait patiently for God's revelations . . . and prepare yourself for the abundance and peace that will most certainly be yours when you do.

A TIMELY TIP FROM THE GARDEN OF LOVE

One of the most important lessons that you can ever learn is to trust God for everything, and that includes timing. In other words, you should trust God to decide the best time for things to happen. Sometimes it's hard to trust God, but it's always the right thing to do.

PROMISES FROM GOD'S WORD

He granted their request because they trusted in Him.

1 CHRONICLES 5:20 HCSB

I know whom I have believed and am persuaded that He is able to guard what has been entrusted to me until that day.

2 TIMOTHY 1:12 HCSB

For the eyes of the Lord range throughout the earth to show Himself strong for those whose hearts are completely His.

2 CHRONICLES 16:9 HCSB

Let us hold fast the confession of our hope without wavering, for He who promised is faithful.

HEBREWS 10:23 NKJV

The one who understands a matter finds success, and the one who trusts in the Lord will be happy.

PROVERBS 16:20 HCSB

MORE GREAT IDEAS

As God's children, we are the recipients of lavish love—a love that motivates us to keep trusting even when we have no idea what God is doing.

BETH MOORE

Earthly fears are no fears at all. Answer the big question of eternity, and the little questions of life fall into perspective.

MAX LUCADO

Are you serious about wanting God's guidance to become the person he wants you to be? The first step is to tell God that you know you can't manage your own life; that you need his help.

CATHERINE MARSHALL

Do not be afraid, then, that if you trust, or tell others to trust, the matter will end there. Trust is only the beginning and the continual foundation. When we trust Him, the Lord works, and His work is the important part of the whole matter.

HANNAH WHITALL SMITH

When the train goes through a tunnel and the world becomes dark, do you jump out? Of course not. You sit still and trust the engineer to get you through.

CORRIE TEN BOOM

Trusting in my own mental understanding becomes a hindrance to complete trust in God.

OSWALD CHAMBERS

Once we recognize our need for Jesus, then the building of our faith begins. It is a daily, moment-by-moment life of absolute dependence upon Him for everything.

CATHERINE MARSHALL

Brother, is your faith looking upward today? / Trust in the promise of the Savior. / Sister, is the light shining bright on your way? / Trust in the promise of thy Lord.

FANNY CROSBY

How happy we are when we realize that He is responsible, that He goes before, that goodness and mercy shall follow us!

MRS. CHARLES E. COWMAN

Never be afraid to trust
an unknown future to
a known God.

—

CORRIE TEN BOOM

A PRAYER FOR TODAY

Dear Lord, as I take the next steps on my life's journey, let me take them with You. Whatever the coming day may bring, I will thank You for the opportunity to live abundantly. I will be Your faith-filled servant, Lord—and I will trust You—this day and forever. Amen

YOUR THOUGHTS ABOUT TRUSTING GOD

_____

_____

_____

_____

_____

_____

_____

_____

_____

_____

_____

_____

CHAPTER

17

ENTRUSTING YOUR HOPES TO GOD

You, Lord, give true peace to those who depend on you, because they trust you.

—

ISAIAH 26:3 NCV

As every woman knows, hope is a perishable commodity. Despite God's promises, despite Christ's love, and despite our countless blessings, we frail human beings can still lose hope from time to time. When we do, we need the encouragement of Christian friends, the life-changing power of prayer, and the healing truth of God's Holy Word. If we find ourselves falling into the spiritual traps of worry and discouragement, we should seek the healing touch of Jesus and the encouraging words of fellow Christians. Even though this world can be a place of trials and struggles, God has promised us peace, joy, and eternal life if we give ourselves to Him.

A TIMELY TIP FROM THE GARDEN OF LOVE

Never be afraid to hope—or to pray—for a miracle.

PROMISES FROM GOD'S WORD

*Let us hold on to the confession of our hope without wavering,
for He who promised is faithful.*

HEBREWS 10:23 HCSB

*Now may the God of hope fill you with all joy and peace in
believing, so that you may overflow with hope by the power of
the Holy Spirit.*

ROMANS 15:13 HCSB

For in You, O Lord, I hope; You will hear, O Lord my God.

PSALM 38:15 NKJV

*I will say to the Lord, "My refuge and my fortress, my God,
in whom I trust."*

PSALM 91:2 HCSB

*The Lord is good to those who wait for Him, to the soul who
seeks Him. It is good that one should hope and wait quietly for
the salvation of the Lord.*

LAMENTATIONS 3:25-26 NKJV

MORE GREAT IDEAS

Easter comes each year to remind us of a truth that is eternal and universal. The empty tomb of Easter morning says to you and me, "Of course you'll encounter trouble. But behold a God of power who can take any evil and turn it into a door of hope."

CATHERINE MARSHALL

How changed our lives would be if we could only fly through the days on wings of surrender and trust!

HANNAH WHITALL SMITH

This hard place in which you perhaps find yourself is the very place in which God is giving you opportunity to look only to Him, to spend time in prayer, and to learn long-suffering, gentleness, meekness—in short, to learn the depths of the love that Christ Himself has poured out on all of us.

ELISABETH ELLIOT

Love is the seed of all hope. It is the enticement to trust, to risk, to try, and to go on.

GLORIA GAITHER

Hope looks for the good in people, opens doors for people, discovers what can be done to help, lights a candle, does not yield to cynicism. Hope sets people free.

BARBARA JOHNSON

The best we can hope for in this life is a knothole peek at the shining realities ahead. Yet a glimpse is enough. It's enough to convince our hearts that whatever sufferings and sorrows currently assail us aren't worthy of comparison to that which waits over the horizon.

JONI EARECKSON TADA

If we just give God the little that we have, we can trust Him to make it go around.

GLORIA GAITHER

The resurrection of Jesus, the whole alphabet of human hope, the certificate of our Lord's mission from heaven, is the heart of the gospel in all ages.

R. G. LEE

Everything that is done in the world is done by hope.

MARTIN LUTHER

Never yield to
gloomy anticipation.
Place your hope and
confidence in God.
He has no record of failure.

—

MRS. CHARLES E. COWMAN

A PRAYER FOR TODAY

Dear Lord, I will place my hope in You. If I become discouraged, I will turn to You. If I am afraid, I will seek strength in You. In every aspect of my life, I will trust You. You are my Father, and I will place my hope, my trust, and my faith in You. Amen

❧

YOUR THOUGHTS ABOUT THE POWER OF HOPE

CHAPTER

18

PEACE FOR
THE JOURNEY

Peace I leave with you, My peace I give to you;
not as the world gives do I give to you.
Let not your heart be troubled,
neither let it be afraid.

—

JOHN 14:27 NKJV

The words of John 14:27 give us hope: "Peace I leave with you, my peace I give unto you . . . ." Jesus offers us peace, not as the world gives, but as He alone gives. We, as believers, can accept His peace or ignore it.

When we accept the peace of Jesus into our hearts, our lives are transformed. And then, because we possess the gift of peace, we can share that gift with fellow Christians, family members, friends, and associates. If, on the other hand, we choose to ignore the gift of peace—for whatever reason—we cannot share what we do not possess.

As every woman knows, peace can be a scarce commodity in our demanding world. How, then, can we find the peace that we so desperately desire? By turning our days and our lives over to God. Elisabeth Elliot writes, "If my life is surrendered to God, all is well. Let me not grab it back, as though it were in peril in His hand but would be safer in mine!" May we give our lives, our hopes, and our prayers to the Lord, and, by doing so, accept His will and His peace.

A TIMELY TIP FROM THE GARDEN OF LOVE

Peace starts at home. You have a big role to play in helping to maintain a peaceful home. It's a big job, so don't be afraid to ask for help . . . especially God's help.

PROMISES FROM GOD'S WORD

Be of good comfort, be of one mind, live in peace; and the God of love and peace will be with you.

2 CORINTHIANS 13:11 NKJV

Now the fruit of righteousness is sown in peace by those who make peace.

JAMES 3:18 NKJV

God has called us to peace.

1 CORINTHIANS 7:15 NKJV

For He is our peace.

EPHESIANS 2:14 HCSB

The result of righteousness will be peace; the effect of righteousness will be quiet confidence forever.

ISAIAH 32:17 HCSB

MORE GREAT IDEAS

Prayer guards hearts and minds and causes God to bring peace out of chaos.

BETH MOORE

When we do what is right, we have contentment, peace, and happiness.

BEVERLY LAHAYE

Peace does not mean to be in a place where there is no noise, trouble, or hard work. Peace means to be in the midst of all those things and still be calm in your heart.

CATHERINE MARSHALL

Christ alone can bring lasting peace—peace with God— peace among men and nations—and peace within our hearts.

BILLY GRAHAM

The fruit of our placing all things in God's hands is the presence of His abiding peace in our hearts.

HANNAH WHITALL SMITH

In the center of a hurricane there is absolute quiet and peace. There is no safer place than in the center of the will of God.

CORRIE TEN BOOM

To know God as He really is—in His essential nature and character—is to arrive at a citadel of peace that circumstances may storm, but can never capture.

CATHERINE MARSHALL

God is in control of history; it's His story. Doesn't that give you a great peace—especially when world events seems so tumultuous and insane?

KAY ARTHUR

Like a spring of pure water, God's peace in our hearts brings cleansing and refreshment to our minds and bodies.

BILLY GRAHAM

When we do what is right, we have contentment, peace, and happiness.

BEVERLY LAHAYE

I believe that in every time and place it is within our power to acquiesce in the will of God—and what peace it brings to do so!

—

ELISABETH ELLIOT

A PRAYER FOR TODAY

Dear Lord, I will open my heart to You. And I thank You, God, for Your love, for Your peace, and for Your Son. Amen

YOUR THOUGHTS ABOUT GOD'S PEACE

_____

_____

_____

_____

_____

_____

_____

_____

_____

_____

_____

_____

_____

HEALTHY RELATIONSHIPS

The one who walks with the wise will become wise,
but a companion of fools will suffer harm.

—

PROVERBS 13:20 HCSB

Emotional health is contagious, and so is emotional distress. If you're fortunate enough to be surrounded by family members and friends who celebrate life and praise God, consider yourself profoundly blessed. But, if you find yourself caught in an unhealthy relationship, it's time to look realistically at your situation and begin making changes.

Don't worry about changing other people: you can't do it. What you can do is to conduct yourself in a responsible fashion and insist that other people treat you with the dignity and consideration that you deserve.

In a perfect world filled with perfect people, our relationships, too, would be perfect. But none of us are perfect and neither are our relationships . . . and that's okay. As we work to make our imperfect relationships a little happier and healthier, we grow as individuals and as families. But, if we find ourselves in relationships that are debilitating or dangerous, then changes must be made, and soon.

God has grand plans for your life; He has promised you the joy and abundance that can be yours through Him. But to fully experience God's gifts, you need happy, emotionally healthy people to share them with. It's up to you to make sure that you do your part to build the kinds of relationships that will bring abundance to you, to your family, and to God's world.

PROMISES FROM GOD'S WORD

A wise man will hear and increase learning, and a man of understanding will attain wise counsel.

PROVERBS 1:5 NKJV

Acquire wisdom—how much better it is than gold! And acquire understanding—it is preferable to silver.

PROVERBS 16:16 HCSB

The one who loves his brother remains in the light, and there is no cause for stumbling in him.

1 JOHN 2:10 HCSB

Now finally, all of you should be like-minded and sympathetic, should love believers, and be compassionate and humble.

1 PETER 3:8 HCSB

A TIMELY TIP FROM THE GARDEN OF LOVE

Sometimes people can be difficult, and sometimes friends misbehave. But it doesn't pay to get angry—your job is to be as understanding as possible. And while you're at it, remember that God wants you to forgive other folks, just like He forgives you.

MORE GREAT IDEAS

Line by line, moment by moment, special times are etched into our memories in the permanent ink of everlasting love in our relationships.

GLORIA GAITHER

It is possible to be close to people physically and miles away from them spiritually.

WARREN WIERSBE

I don't buy the cliché that quality time is the most important thing. If you don't have enough quantity, you won't get quality.

LEIGHTON FORD

When you extend hospitality to others, you're not trying to impress people, you're trying to reflect God to them.

MAX LUCADO

When we Christians are too busy to care for each other, we're simply too busy for our own good . . . and for God's.

MARIE T. FREEMAN

Make it a rule, and pray to God to help you to keep it, never, if possible, to lie down at night without being able to say: "I have made one human being at least a little wiser, or a little happier, or at least a little better this day."

CHARLES KINGSLEY

Friendships are living organisms at work. They continue to unfold, change, and emerge.

BARBARA JOHNSON

When something robs you of your peace of mind, ask yourself if it is worth the energy you are expending on it. If not, then put it out of your mind in an act of discipline. Every time the thought of "it" returns, refuse it.

KAY ARTHUR

It doesn't take monumental feats to make the world a better place. It can be as simple as letting someone go ahead of you in a grocery line.

BARBARA JOHNSON

True friendship can harbor no suspicion; a friend must speak to a friend as freely as to his second self.

ST. JEROME

A person who really cares
about his or her neighbor,
a person who genuinely loves
others, is a person who bears
witness to the truth.

—

ANNE GRAHAM LOTZ

A PRAYER FOR TODAY

Dear Lord, You have brought family members and friends into my life. Let me love them, let me help them, let me treasure them, and let me lead them to You. Amen

❧

YOUR THOUGHTS ABOUT HEALTHY RELATIONSHIPS

_____

_____

_____

_____

_____

_____

_____

_____

_____

_____

_____

_____

_____

20

ENDURING
TOUGH TIMES

*We are pressured in every way but not crushed;
we are perplexed but not in despair.*

—

2 CORINTHIANS 4:8 HCSB

Women of every generation have experienced adversity, and this generation is no different. But, today's women face challenges that previous generations could have scarcely imagined. Thankfully, although the world continues to change, God's love remains constant. And, He remains ready to comfort us and strengthen us whenever we turn to Him.

Psalm 147 promises, "He heals the brokenhearted, and binds their wounds" (v. 3). When we are troubled, we must call upon God, and, in His own time and according to His own plan, He will heal us.

If you are like most women, it is simply a fact of life: from time to time, you worry. You worry about health, about finances, about safety, about relationships, about family, and about countless other challenges of life, some great and some small. Where is the best place to take your worries? Take them to God. Seek protection from the One who cannot be moved.

A TIMELY TIP FROM THE GARDEN OF LOVE

If you're facing big-time adversity, don't hit the panic button and don't keep everything bottled up inside. Instead of going underground, talk things over with your husband, with your friends, with your pastor, and if necessary, with a trained counselor. When it comes to navigating the stormy seas of life, second, third, fourth, or even fifth opinions can sometimes be helpful.

PROMISES FROM GOD'S WORD

I will be with you when you pass through the waters . . . when you walk through the fire . . . the flame will not burn you. For I the Lord your God, the Holy One of Israel, and your Savior.

ISAIAH 43:2-3 HCSB

But as for you, you meant evil against me; but God meant it for good, in order to bring it about as it is this day, to save many people alive.

GENESIS 50:20 NKJV

I called to the Lord in my distress; I called to my God. From His temple He heard my voice.

2 SAMUEL 22:7 HCSB

When you are in distress and all these things have happened to you, you will return to the Lord your God in later days and obey Him. He will not leave you, destroy you, or forget the covenant with your fathers that He swore to them by oath, because the Lord your God is a compassionate God.

DEUTERONOMY 4:30-31 HCSB

MORE GREAT IDEAS

When faced with adversity the Christian woman comforts herself with the knowledge that all of life's events are in the hands of God.

VONETTE BRIGHT

God whispers to us in our pleasures, speaks in our conscience, but shouts in our pain.

C. S. LEWIS

The only way to learn a strong faith is to endure great trials. I have learned my faith by standing firm amid the most severe of tests.

GEORGE MUELLER

If all struggles and sufferings were eliminated, the spirit would no more reach maturity than would the child.

ELISABETH ELLIOT

Faith is a strong power, mastering any difficulty in the strength of the Lord who made heaven and earth.

CORRIE TEN BOOM

Even in the winter, even in the midst of the storm, the sun is still there. Somewhere, up above the clouds, it still shines and warms and pulls at the life buried deep inside the brown branches and frozen earth. The sun is there! Spring will come.

GLORIA GAITHER

God will never let you sink under your circumstances. He always provides a safety net and His love always encircles.

BARBARA JOHNSON

When problems threaten to engulf us, we must do what believers have always done, turn to the Lord for encouragement and solace. As Psalm 46:1 states, "God is our refuge and strength, an ever-present help in trouble."

SHIRLEY DOBSON

God helps those who help themselves, but there are times when we are quite incapable of helping ourselves. That's when God stoops down and gathers us in His arms like a mother lifts a sick child, and does for us what we cannot do for ourselves.

RUTH BELL GRAHAM

Measure the size of the obstacles against the size of God.

—

BETH MOORE

A PRAYER FOR TODAY

Dear Heavenly Father, when I am troubled, You heal me. When I am afraid, You protect me. When I am discouraged, You lift me up. You are my unending source of strength, Lord; let me turn to You when I am weak. In times of adversity, let me trust Your plan and Your will for my life. And whatever my circumstances, Lord, let me always give the thanks and the glory to You. Amen

YOUR THOUGHTS ABOUT DEALING WITH TOUGH TIMES

_____

_____

_____

_____

_____

_____

_____

_____

_____

_____

CHAPTER

21

THIS IS THE DAY

This is the day the LORD has made;
we will rejoice and be glad in it.

—

PSALM 118:24 NKJV

The words of Psalm 118:24 remind us of a profound yet simple truth: God created this day, and it's up to each of us to rejoice and to be grateful.

For Christian believers, every day begins and ends with God and His Son. Christ came to this earth to give us abundant life and eternal salvation. We give thanks to our Maker when we treasure each day and use it to the fullest.

This day is a gift from God. How will you use it? Will you celebrate God's gifts and obey His commandments? Will you share words of encouragement and hope with all who cross your path? Will you share the Good News of the risen Christ? Will you trust in the Father and praise His glorious handiwork? The answer to these questions will determine, to a surprising extent, the direction and the quality of your day.

So whatever this day holds for you, begin it and end it with God as your partner and Christ as your Savior. And throughout the day, give thanks to the One who created you and saved you. God's love for you is infinite. Accept it joyously and be thankful.

A TIMELY TIP FROM THE GARDEN OF LOVE

If you don't feel like celebrating, start counting your blessings. Before long, you'll realize that you have plenty of reasons to celebrate.

PROMISES FROM GOD'S WORD

I must work the works of Him who sent Me while it is day; the night is coming when no one can work.

JOHN 9:4 NKJV

But encourage each other daily, while it is still called today, so that none of you is hardened by sin's deception.

HEBREWS 3:13 HCSB

Working together with Him, we also appeal to you: "Don't receive God's grace in vain." For He says: In an acceptable time, I heard you, and in the day of salvation, I helped you. Look, now is the acceptable time; look, now is the day of salvation.

2 CORINTHIANS 6:1-2 HCSB

Therefore, get your minds ready for action, being self-disciplined, and set your hope completely on the grace to be brought to you at the revelation of Jesus Christ.

1 PETER 1:13 HCSB

Rejoice in the Lord always. I will say it again: Rejoice!

PHILIPPIANS 4:4 HCSB

151

MORE GREAT IDEAS

Jesus intended for us to be overwhelmed by the blessings of regular days. He said it was the reason he had come: "I am come that they might have life, and that they might have it more abundantly."

GLORIA GAITHER

Yesterday is the tomb of time, and tomorrow is the womb of time. Only now is yours.

R. G. LEE

God gave you this glorious day. Don't disappoint Him. Use it for His glory.

MARIE T. FREEMAN

When the dream of our heart is one that God has planted there, a strange happiness flows into us. At that moment, all of the spiritual resources of the universe are released to help us. Our praying is then at one with the will of God and becomes a channel for the Creator's purposes for us and our world.

CATHERINE MARSHALL

If you can forgive the person you were, accept the person you are, and believe in the person you will become, you are headed for joy. So celebrate your life.

BARBARA JOHNSON

If we are ever going to be or do anything for our Lord, now is the time.

VANCE HAVNER

Christ is the secret, the source, the substance, the center, and the circumference of all true and lasting gladness.

MRS. CHARLES E. COWMAN

Submit each day to God, knowing that He is God over all your tomorrows.

KAY ARTHUR

Trusting God completely means having faith that he knows what is best for your life. You expect him to keep his promises, help you with problems, and do the impossible when necessary.

RICK WARREN

Claim the joy that is yours. Pray.
And know that your joy
is used by God to reach others.

—

KAY ARTHUR

A PRAYER FOR TODAY

Dear Lord, You have given me another day of life; let me celebrate this day, and let me use it according to Your plan. I come to You today with faith in my heart and praise on my lips. I praise You, Father, for the gift of life and for the friends and family members who make my life rich. Enable me to live each moment to the fullest, totally involved in Your will. Amen

YOUR THOUGHTS ABOUT THE NEED TO CELEBRATE EACH DAY

CHAPTER

22

MAINTAINING PERSPECTIVE

Make your own attitude that of Christ Jesus.

—

PHILIPPIANS 2:5 HCSB

Sometimes, amid the demands of daily life, we lose perspective. Life seems out of balance, and the pressures of everyday living seem overwhelming. What's needed is a fresh perspective, a restored sense of balance . . . and God.

If a temporary loss of perspective has left you worried, exhausted, or both, it's time to readjust your thought patterns. Negative thoughts are habit-forming; thankfully, so are positive ones. With practice, you can form the habit of focusing on God's priorities and your possibilities. When you do, you'll soon discover that you will spend less time fretting about your challenges and more time praising God for His gifts.

When you call upon the Lord and prayerfully seek His will, He will give you wisdom and perspective. When you make God's priorities your priorities, He will direct your steps and calm your fears. So today and every day hereafter, pray for a sense of balance and perspective. And remember: your thoughts are intensely powerful things, so handle them with care.

A TIMELY TIP FROM THE GARDEN OF LOVE

Keep things in perspective. Your life is an integral part of God's grand plan. So don't become unduly upset over the minor inconveniences of life, and don't worry too much about today's setbacks—they're temporary.

PROMISES FROM GOD'S WORD

Set your minds on what is above, not on what is on the earth.

COLOSSIANS 3:2 HCSB

But Martha was distracted by her many tasks, and she came up and asked, "Lord, don't You care that my sister has left me to serve alone? So tell her to give me a hand." The Lord answered her, "Martha, Martha, you are worried and upset about many things, but one thing is necessary. Mary has made the right choice, and it will not be taken away from her."

LUKE 10:40-42 HCSB

Finally brothers, whatever is true, whatever is honorable, whatever is just, whatever is pure, whatever is lovely, whatever is commendable—if there is any moral excellence and if there is any praise—dwell on these things.

PHILIPPIANS 4:8 HCSB

For the word of God is living and powerful, and sharper than any two-edged sword, piercing even to the division of soul and spirit, and of joints and marrow, and is a discerner of the thoughts and intents of the heart.

HEBREWS 4:12 NKJV

MORE GREAT IDEAS

When the dream of our heart is one that God has planted there, a strange happiness flows into us. At that moment, all of the spiritual resources of the universe are released to help us. Our praying is then at one with the will of God and becomes a channel for the Creator's purposes for us and our world.

CATHERINE MARSHALL

Earthly fears are no fears at all. Answer the big questions of eternity, and the little questions of life fall into perspective.

MAX LUCADO

What you see and hear depends a good deal on where you are standing; it also depends on what sort of person you are.

C. S. LEWIS

Like a shadow declining swiftly . . . away . . . like the dew of the morning gone with the heat of the day; like the wind in the treetops, like a wave of the sea, so are our lives on earth when seen in light of eternity.

RUTH BELL GRAHAM

Don't be addicted to approval. Follow your heart. Do what you believe God is telling you to do, and stand firm in Him and Him alone.

JOYCE MEYER

The proper perspective creates within us a spirit of reaching outside of ourselves with joy and enthusiasm.

LUCI SWINDOLL

Instead of being frustrated and overwhelmed by all that is going on in our world, go to the Lord and ask Him to give you His eternal perspective.

KAY ARTHUR

Obey God one step at a time, then the next step will come into view.

CATHERINE MARSHALL

Attitude is the mind's paintbrush;
it can color any situation.

—

BARBARA JOHNSON

A PRAYER FOR TODAY

Dear Lord, give me wisdom and perspective. Guide me according to Your plans for my life and according to Your commandments. And keep me mindful, Dear Lord, that Your truth is—and will forever be—the ultimate truth. Amen

YOUR THOUGHTS ABOUT KEEPING THINGS IN PERSPECTIVE

_____

_____

_____

_____

_____

_____

_____

_____

_____

_____

_____

_____

CHAPTER

23

ACCEPTING GOD'S ABUNDANCE

I am come that they might have life,
and that they might have it more abundantly.

—

JOHN 10:10 KJV

The familiar words of John 10:10 should serve as a daily reminder: Christ came to this earth so that we might experience His abundance, His love, and His gift of eternal life. But Christ does not force Himself upon us; we must claim His gifts for ourselves.

Every woman knows that some days are so busy and so hurried that abundance seems a distant promise. It is not. Every day, we can claim the spiritual abundance that God promises for our lives . . . and we should.

Thomas Brooks spoke for believers of every generation when he observed, "Christ is the sun, and all the watches of our lives should be set by the dial of his motion." Christ, indeed, is the ultimate Savior of mankind and the personal Savior of those who believe in Him. As His servants, we should place Him at the very center of our lives. And, every day that God gives us breath, we should share Christ's love and His abundance with a world that needs both.

A TIMELY TIP FROM THE GARDEN OF LOVE

God wants to shower you with abundance—your job is to let Him.

PROMISES FROM GOD'S WORD

And God is able to make every grace overflow to you, so that in every way, always having everything you need, you may excel in every good work.

2 CORINTHIANS 9:8 HCSB

And He said to them, "Take heed and beware of covetousness, for one's life does not consist in the abundance of the things he possesses."

LUKE 12:15 NKJV

Until now you have asked for nothing in My name. Ask and you will receive, that your joy may be complete.

JOHN 16:24 HCSB

My cup runs over. Surely goodness and mercy shall follow me all the days of my life; and I will dwell in the house of the Lord forever.

PSALM 23:5-6 NKJV

Come to terms with God and be at peace; in this way good will come to you.

JOB 22:21 HCSB

MORE GREAT IDEAS

God has promised us abundance, peace, and eternal life. These treasures are ours for the asking; all we must do is claim them. One of the great mysteries of life is why on earth do so many of us wait so very long to lay claim to God's gifts?

MARIE T. FREEMAN

Yes, we were created for His holy pleasure, but we will ultimately—if not immediately—find much pleasure in His pleasure.

BETH MOORE

Get ready for God to show you not only His pleasure, but His approval.

JONI EARECKSON TADA

Jesus intended for us to be overwhelmed by the blessings of regular days. He said it was the reason he had come: "I am come that they might have life, and that they might have it more abundantly."

GLORIA GAITHER

The gift of God is eternal life, spiritual life, abundant life through faith in Jesus Christ, the Living Word of God.

ANNE GRAHAM LOTZ

It would be wrong to have a "poverty complex," for to think ourselves paupers is to deny either the King's riches or to deny our being His children.

CATHERINE MARSHALL

God loves you and wants you to experience peace and life—abundant and eternal.

BILLY GRAHAM

Don't be afraid to ask your heavenly Father for anything you need. Indeed, nothing is too small for God's attention or too great for his power.

DENNIS SWANBERG

God is the giver, and we are the receivers. And His richest gifts are bestowed not upon those who do the greatest things, but upon those who accept His abundance and His grace.

HANNAH WHITALL SMITH

God's riches are beyond
anything we could ask or
even dare to imagine!
If my life gets gooey and stale,
I have no excuse.

—

BARBARA JOHNSON

A PRAYER FOR TODAY

Dear Lord, thank You for the joyful, abundant life that is mine through Christ Jesus. Guide me according to Your will, and help me become a woman whose life is a worthy example to others. Give me courage, Lord, to claim the spiritual riches that You have promised, and show me Your plan for my life, today and forever. Amen

ॐ

YOUR THOUGHTS ABOUT GOD'S ABUNDANCE

THANKSGIVING NOW

In everything give thanks;
for this is the will of God in Christ Jesus for you.

—

1 THESSALONIANS 5:18 NKJV

As busy women caught up in the inevitable demands of everyday life, we sometimes fail to pause and thank our Creator for the countless blessings He has bestowed upon us. And that's unfortunate because, as believing Christians, we are blessed beyond measure.

God sent His only Son to die for our sins. And, God has given us the priceless gifts of eternal love and eternal life. We, in turn, are instructed to approach our Heavenly Father with reverence and thanksgiving.

When we slow down and express our gratitude to the One who made us, we enrich our own lives and the lives of those around us. Thanksgiving should become a habit, a regular part of our daily routines. Yes, God has blessed us beyond measure, and we owe Him everything.

A TIMELY TIP FROM THE GARDEN OF LOVE

You owe God everything . . . including your thanks. So, start right now.

PROMISES FROM GOD'S WORD

Therefore as you have received Christ Jesus the Lord, walk in Him, rooted and built up in Him and established in the faith, just as you were taught, and overflowing with thankfulness.

COLOSSIANS 2:6-7 HCSB

Give thanks to the Lord, for He is good; His faithful love endures forever.

PSALM 106:1 HCSB

Thanks be to God for His indescribable gift.

2 CORINTHIANS 9:15 HCSB

Enter into His gates with thanksgiving, and into His courts with praise. Be thankful to Him, and bless His name. For the Lord is good; His mercy is everlasting, and His truth endures to all generations.

PSALM 100:4-5 NKJV

And whatever you do, in word or in deed, do everything in the name of the Lord Jesus, giving thanks to God the Father through Him.

COLOSSIANS 3:17 HCSB

MORE GREAT IDEAS

Do you know that if at birth I had been able to make one petition, it would have been that I should be born blind? Because, when I get to heaven, the first face that shall ever gladden my sight will be that of my Savior!

FANNY CROSBY

Thanksgiving is good but Thanksliving is better.

JIM GALLERY

Words fail to express my love for this holy Book, my gratitude for its author, for His love and goodness. How shall I thank him for it?

LOTTIE MOON

It is only with gratitude that life becomes rich.

DIETRICH BONHOEFFER

God is worthy of our praise and is pleased when we come before Him with thanksgiving.

SHIRLEY DOBSON

173

It is always possible to be thankful for what is given rather than to complain about what is not given. One or the other becomes a habit of life.

ELISABETH ELLIOT

Thanksgiving or complaining—these words express two contrastive attitudes of the souls of God's children in regard to His dealings with them. The soul that gives thanks can find comfort in everything; the soul that complains can find comfort in nothing.

HANNAH WHITALL SMITH

If you pause to think—you'll have cause to thank!

ANONYMOUS

God has promised that if we harvest well with the tools of thanksgiving, there will be seeds for planting in the spring.

GLORIA GAITHER

The words "thank" and "think" come from the same root word. If we would think more, we would thank more.

WARREN WIERSBE

The act of thanksgiving is
a demonstration of the fact
that you are going to
trust and believe God.

—

KAY ARTHUR

A PRAYER FOR TODAY

Dear Lord, I'm really thankful for all the good things I have. Today I will show You how grateful I am, not only by the words that I speak, but also by the way that I act. Amen

MAKE A LIST OF THINGS
TO BE THANKFUL FOR

_____

_____

_____

_____

_____

_____

_____

_____

_____

_____

_____

_____

_____

CHAPTER

25

CONTINUING
TO GROW

*For this reason also, since the day we heard this,
we haven't stopped praying for you.
We are asking that you may be filled with
the knowledge of His will in all wisdom and
spiritual understanding.*

—

COLOSSIANS 1:9 HCSB

When will you be a "fully-grown" Christian woman? Hopefully never—or at least not until you arrive in heaven! As a believer living here on planet earth, you're never "fully grown"; you always have the potential to keep growing.

Many of life's most important lessons are painful to learn, but spiritual growth need not take place only in times of pain and hardship. Whatever your circumstances, God is always standing at the door; whenever you are ready to reach out to Him, He will answer.

In those quiet moments when you open your heart to God, the One who made you keeps remaking you. He gives you direction, perspective, wisdom, and courage. And, the appropriate moment to accept those spiritual gifts is always the present one.

Would you like a time-tested formula for spiritual growth? Here it is: keep studying God's Word, keep obeying His commandments, keep praying (and listening for answers), and seek to live in the center of God's will. When you do, you will never be a "stagnant" believer. You will, instead, be a growing Christian . . . and that's precisely the kind of Christian God wants you to be.

A TIMELY TIP FROM THE GARDEN OF LOVE

Spiritual maturity is a journey, not a destination. A growing relationship with God should be your highest priority.

PROMISES FROM GOD'S WORD

I want their hearts to be encouraged and joined together in love, so that they may have all the riches of assured understanding, and have the knowledge of God's mystery—Christ.

COLOSSIANS 2:2 HCSB

For though by this time you ought to be teachers, you need someone to teach you again the basic principles of God's revelation. You need milk, not solid food. Now everyone who lives on milk is inexperienced with the message about righteousness, because he is an infant. But solid food is for the mature—for those whose senses have been trained to distinguish between good and evil.

HEBREWS 5:12-14 HCSB

But grow in the grace and knowledge of our Lord and Savior Jesus Christ. To Him be the glory both now and to the day of eternity.

2 PETER 3:18 HCSB

Therefore, leaving the elementary message about the Messiah, let us go on to maturity.

HEBREWS 6:1 HCSB

179

MORE GREAT IDEAS

Growth in depth and strength and consistency and fruitfulness and ultimately in Christlikeness is only possible when the winds of life are contrary to personal comfort.

ANNE GRAHAM LOTZ

We set our eyes on the finish line, forgetting the past, and straining toward the mark of spiritual maturity and fruitfulness.

VONETTE BRIGHT

God is teaching me to become more and more "teachable": To keep evolving. To keep taking the risk of learning something new . . . or unlearning something old and off base.

BETH MOORE

We look at our burdens and heavy loads, and we shrink from them. But, if we lift them and bind them about our hearts, they become wings, and on them we can rise and soar toward God.

MRS. CHARLES E. COWMAN

If all struggles and sufferings were eliminated, the spirit would no more reach maturity than would the child.

ELISABETH ELLIOT

You are either becoming more like Christ every day or you're becoming less like Him. There is no neutral position in the Lord.

STORMIE OMARTIAN

Aim at Heaven and you will get earth "thrown in"; aim at earth and you will get neither.

C. S. LEWIS

He makes us wait. He keeps us in the dark on purpose. He makes us walk when we want to run, sit still when we want to walk, for he has things to do in our souls that we are not interested in.

ELISABETH ELLIOT

There is wonderful freedom and joy in coming to recognize that the fun is in the becoming.

GLORIA GAITHER

Grow, dear friends, but grow,
I beseech you, in God's way,
which is the only true way.

—

HANNAH WHITALL SMITH

A PRAYER FOR TODAY

Lord, help me to keep growing spiritually and emotionally. Let me live according to Your Word, and let me grow in my faith every day that I live. Amen

❧

YOUR THOUGHTS ABOUT SPIRITUAL GROWTH

_____

_____

_____

_____

_____

_____

_____

_____

_____

_____

_____

_____

_____

CHAPTER

26

THE GIFT OF ENCOURAGEMENT

I want their hearts to be encouraged and
joined together in love, so that they may have
all the riches of assured understanding,
and have the knowledge of God's mystery—Christ.

COLOSSIANS 2:2 HCSB

Are you a woman who is a continuing source of encouragement to your family and friends? Hopefully so. After all, one of the reasons that God put you here is to serve and encourage other people—starting with the people who live under your roof.

In his letter to the Ephesians, Paul writes, "Do not let any unwholesome talk come out of your mouths, but only what is helpful for building others up according to their needs, that it may benefit those who listen" (4:29 NIV). This passage reminds us that, as Christians, we are instructed to choose our words carefully so as to build others up through wholesome, honest encouragement. How can we build others up? By celebrating their victories and their accomplishments. As the old saying goes, "When someone does something good, applaud—you'll make two people happy."

Today, look for the good in others and celebrate the good that you find. When you do, you'll be a powerful force of encouragement in your corner of the world . . . and a worthy servant to your God.

A TIMELY TIP FROM THE GARDEN OF LOVE

Encouragement is contagious. You can't lift other people up without lifting yourself up, too.

PROMISES FROM GOD'S WORD

But encourage each other daily, while it is still called today, so that none of you is hardened by sin's deception.

HEBREWS 3:13 HCSB

So then, we must pursue what promotes peace and what builds up one another.

ROMANS 14:19 HCSB

Carry one another's burdens; in this way you will fulfill the law of Christ.

GALATIANS 6:2 HCSB

And let us be concerned about one another in order to promote love and good works.

HEBREWS 10:24 HCSB

Anxiety in a man's heart weighs it down, but a good word cheers it up.

PROVERBS 12:25 HCSB

MORE GREAT IDEAS

Don't forget that a single sentence, spoken at the right moment, can change somebody's whole perspective on life. A little encouragement can go a long, long way.

MARIE T. FREEMAN

Encouragement starts at home, but it should never end there.

MARIE T. FREEMAN

Words. Do you fully understand their power? Can any of us really grasp the mighty force behind the things we say? Do we stop and think before we speak, considering the potency of the words we utter?

JONI EARECKSON TADA

The glory of friendship is not the outstretched hand, or the kindly smile, or the joy of companionship. It is the spiritual inspiration that comes to one when he discovers that someone else believes in him and is willing to trust him with his friendship.

CORRIE TEN BOOM

Always stay connected to people and seek out things that bring you joy. Dream with abandon. Pray confidently.

BARBARA JOHNSON

If I am asked how we are to get rid of discouragements, I can only say, as I have had to say of so many other wrong spiritual habits, we must give them up. It is never worthwhile to argue against discouragement. There is only one argument that can meet it, and that is the argument of God.

HANNAH WHITALL SMITH

I can usually sense that a leading is from the Holy Spirit when it calls me to humble myself, to serve somebody, to encourage somebody, or to give something away. Very rarely will the evil one lead us to do those kind of things.

BILL HYBELS

One of the ways God refills us after failure is through the blessing of Christian fellowship. Just experiencing the joy of simple activities shared with other children of God can have a healing effect on us.

ANNE GRAHAM LOTZ

A single word, if spoken
in a friendly spirit, may be
sufficient to turn one
from dangerous error.

—

FANNY CROSBY

A PRAYER FOR TODAY

Dear Heavenly Father, because I am Your child, I am blessed. You have loved me eternally, cared for me faithfully, and saved me through the gift of Your Son Jesus. Just as You have lifted me up, Lord, let me lift up others in a spirit of encouragement and optimism and hope. And, if I can help a fellow traveler, even in a small way, Dear Lord, may the glory be Yours. Amen

❧

YOUR THOUGHTS ABOUT THE IMPORTANCE OF ENCOURAGEMENT

_____

_____

_____

_____

_____

_____

_____

_____

_____

CHAPTER

27

ABOVE AND BEYOND WORRY

*Don't worry about your life, what you will
eat or what you will drink; or about your body,
what you will wear. Isn't life more than food and
the body more than clothing?*

—

MATTHEW 6:25 HCSB

If you are like most women, it is simply a fact of life: from time to time, you worry. You worry about health, about finances, about safety, about relationships, about family, and about countless other challenges of life, some great and some small. Where is the best place to take your worries? Take them to God. Take your troubles to Him, and your fears, and your sorrows.

Barbara Johnson correctly observed, "Worry is the senseless process of cluttering up tomorrow's opportunities with leftover problems from today." So if you'd like to make the most out of this day (and every one hereafter), turn your worries over to a Power greater than yourself . . . and spend your valuable time and energy solving the problems you can fix . . . while trusting God to do the rest.

A TIMELY TIP FROM THE GARDEN OF LOVE

An important part of becoming a more mature Christian is learning to worry less and to trust God more.

PROMISES FROM GOD'S WORD

Therefore don't worry about tomorrow, because tomorrow will worry about itself. Each day has enough trouble of its own.

MATTHEW 6:34 HCSB

Anxiety in a man's heart weighs it down, but a good word cheers it up.

PROVERBS 12:25 HCSB

Don't worry about anything, but in everything, through prayer and petition with thanksgiving, let your requests be made known to God.

PHILIPPIANS 4:6 HCSB

Yea, though I walk through the valley of the shadow of death, I will fear no evil: for thou art with me; thy rod and thy staff they comfort me.

PSALM 23:4 KJV

MORE GREAT IDEAS

Worry is a cycle of inefficient thoughts whirling around a center of fear.

CORRIE TEN BOOM

This life of faith, then, consists in just this—being a child in the Father's house. Let the ways of childish confidence and freedom from care, which so please you and win your heart when you observe your own little ones, teach you what you should be in your attitude toward God.

HANNAH WHITALL SMITH

When there is perplexity there is always guidance—not always at the moment we ask, but in good time, which is God's time. There is no need to fret and stew.

ELISABETH ELLIOT

In those desperate times when we feel like we don't have an ounce of strength, He will gently pick up our heads so that our eyes can behold something—something that will keep His hope alive in us.

KATHY TROCCOLI

We are not called to be burden-bearers, but cross-bearers and light-bearers. We must cast our burdens on the Lord.

CORRIE TEN BOOM

Never yield to gloomy anticipation. Place your hope and confidence in God. He has no record of failure.

MRS. CHARLES E. COWMAN

The happiest people in the world are not those who have no problems, but the people who have learned to live with those things that are less than perfect.

JAMES DOBSON

Anxiety may be natural and normal for the world, but it is not to be part of a believer's lifestyle.

KAY ARTHUR

Today is mine. Tomorrow is none of my business. If I peer anxiously into the fog of the future, I will strain my spiritual eyes so that I will not see clearly what is required of me now.

ELISABETH ELLIOTT

Worry is the senseless process
of cluttering up tomorrow's
opportunities with leftover
problems from today.

—

BARBARA JOHNSON

A PRAYER FOR TODAY

Dear Lord, wherever I find myself, let me celebrate more and worry less. When my faith begins to waver, help me to trust You more. Then, with praise on my lips and the love of Your Son in my heart, let me live courageously, faithfully, prayerfully, and thankfully this day and every day. Amen

❧

YOUR THOUGHTS ABOUT WORRIES

CHAPTER

28

YOUR SHEPHERD

The Lord is my shepherd; I shall not want.

—

PSALM 23:1 KJV

Because we are imperfect human beings living imperfect lives, we worry. Even though we, as Christians, have the assurance of salvation—even though we, as believers, have the promise of God's love and protection—we find ourselves fretting over the countless details of everyday life. Jesus understood our concerns, and He addressed them.

In the 6th chapter of Matthew, Jesus makes it clear that the heart of God is a protective, caring heart:

> *Therefore I say to you, do not worry about your life, what you will eat or what you will drink; nor about your body, what you will put on. Is not life more than food and the body more than clothing? Look at the birds of the air, for they neither sow nor reap nor gather into barns; yet your heavenly Father feeds them. Are you not of more value than they? Which of you by worrying can add one cubit to his stature? . . . Therefore do not worry about tomorrow, for tomorrow will worry about its own things. Sufficient for the day is its own trouble. (vv. 25-27, 34)*

Perhaps you are uncertain about your future, your finances, your relationships, or your health. Or perhaps you are simply a "worrier" by nature. If so, make Matthew 6 a regular part of your daily Bible reading. This beautiful passage will remind you that God still sits in His heaven and you are His beloved child. Then, perhaps, you will worry a little less and trust God a little more, and that's as it should be because God is trustworthy . . . and you are protected.

THE 23RD PSALM

The LORD is my shepherd; I shall not want.
He maketh me to lie down in green pastures:
he leadeth me beside the still waters. He restoreth my soul:
he leadeth me in the paths of righteousness for his name's sake.
Yea, though I walk through the valley of the shadow of death,
I will fear no evil: for thou art with me; thy rod and thy staff
they comfort me. Thou preparest a table before me in
the presence of mine enemies: thou anointest my head
with oil; my cup runneth over. Surely goodness and
mercy shall follow me all the days of my life:
and I will dwell in the house of the LORD for ever.

PROMISES FROM GOD'S WORD

Finally, my brethren, be strong in the Lord and in the power of His might. Put on the whole armor of God, that you may be able to stand against the wiles of the devil.

EPHESIANS 6:10-11 NKJV

But the Lord will be a refuge for His people.

JOEL 3:16 HCSB

The Lord your God in your midst, The Mighty One, will save; He will rejoice over you with gladness, He will quiet you with His love, He will rejoice over you with singing.

ZEPHANIAH 3:17 NKJV

I know whom I have believed and am persuaded that He is able to guard what has been entrusted to me until that day.

2 TIMOTHY 1:12 HCSB

A TIMELY TIP FROM THE GARDEN OF LOVE

You are protected by God . . . now and always. The only security that lasts is the security that flows from the loving heart of God.

MORE GREAT IDEAS

The Rock of Ages is the great sheltering encirclement.

OSWALD CHAMBERS

Our future may look fearfully intimidating, yet we can look up to the Engineer of the Universe, confident that nothing escapes His attention or slips out of the control of those strong hands.

ELISABETH ELLIOT

We are never out of reach of Satan's devices, so we must never be without the whole armor of God.

WARREN WIERSBE

Only believe, don't fear. Our Master, Jesus, always watches over us, and no matter what the persecution, Jesus will surely overcome it.

LOTTIE MOON

God will never let you sink under your circumstances. He always provide a safety net and His love always encircles.

BARBARA JOHNSON

A God wise enough to create me and the world I live in is wise enough to watch out for me.

PHILIP YANCEY

Worries carry responsibilities that belong to God, not to you. Worry does not enable us to escape evil; it makes us unfit to cope with it when it comes.

CORRIE TEN BOOM

As sure as God puts his children in the furnace, he will be in the furnace with them.

C. H. SPURGEON

Seeing that a Pilot steers the ship in which we sail, who will never allow us to perish even in the midst of shipwrecks, there is no reason why our minds should be overwhelmed with fear and overcome with weariness.

JOHN CALVIN

We have ample evidence that the Lord is able to guide. The promises cover every imaginable situation. All we need to do is to take the hand he stretches out.

ELISABETH ELLIOT

It is wonderful to have all kinds
of human support systems,
but we must always stand firm
in God and in Him alone.

—

JOYCE MEYER

A PRAYER FOR TODAY

Lord, You have promised to protect me, and I will trust You. Today, I will live courageously as I place my hopes, my faith, and life in Your hands. Let my life be a testimony to the transforming power of Your love, Your grace, and Your Son. Amen

∽

YOUR THOUGHTS ABOUT GOD'S PROTECTION

ENTHUSIASM
FOR THE JOURNEY

Whatever you do, do it enthusiastically,
as something done for the Lord and not for men.

—

COLOSSIANS 3:23 HCSB

Can you truthfully say that you are an enthusiastic person? Are you passionate about your faith, your life, your family, and your future? Hopefully so. But if your zest for life has waned, it is now time to redirect your efforts and recharge your spiritual batteries. And that means refocusing your priorities by putting God first.

Each day is a glorious opportunity to serve God and to do His will. Are you enthused about life, or do you struggle through each day giving scarcely a thought to God's blessings? Are you constantly praising God for His gifts, and are you sharing His Good News with the world? And are you excited about the possibilities for service that God has placed before you, whether at home, at work, or at church? You should be.

Nothing is more important than your wholehearted commitment to your Creator and to His only begotten Son. Your faith must never be an afterthought; it must be your ultimate priority, your ultimate possession, and your ultimate passion. When you become passionate about your faith, you'll become passionate about your life, too.

Norman Vincent Peale advised, "Get absolutely enthralled with something. Throw yourself into it with abandon. Get out of yourself. Be somebody. Do something." His words apply to you. So don't settle for a lukewarm existence. Instead, make the character-building choice to become genuinely involved in life. The world needs your enthusiasm . . . and so do you.

PROMISES FROM GOD'S WORD

Do not lack diligence; be fervent in spirit; serve the Lord.

ROMANS 12:11 HCSB

Render service with a good attitude, as to the Lord and not to men . . .

EPHESIANS 6:7 HCSB

I have seen that there is nothing better than for a person to enjoy his activities, because that is his reward. For who can enable him to see what will happen after he dies?

ECCLESIASTES 3:22 HCSB

He did it with all his heart. So he prospered.

2 CHRONICLES 31:21 NKJV

A TIMELY TIP FROM THE GARDEN OF LOVE

Don't wait for enthusiasm to find you . . . go looking for it. Look at your life and your relationships as exciting adventures. Don't wait for life to spice up itself; spice things up yourself.

MORE GREAT IDEAS

Enthusiasm, like the flu, is contagious—we get it from one another.

BARBARA JOHNSON

Your light is the truth of the Gospel message itself as well as your witness as to Who Jesus is and what He has done for you. Don't hide it.

ANNE GRAHAM LOTZ

Living life with a consistent spiritual walk deeply influences those we love most.

VONETTE BRIGHT

We urgently need people who encourage and inspire us to move toward God and away from the world's enticing pleasures.

JIM CYMBALA

Catch on fire with enthusiasm and people will come for miles to watch you burn.

JOHN WESLEY

I don't know about you, but I want to do more than survive life—I want to mount up like the eagle and glide over rocky crags, nest in the tallest of trees, dive for nourishment in the deepest of mountain lakes, and soar on the wings of the wind.

BARBARA JOHNSON

Those who are fired with an enthusiastic idea and who allow it to take hold and dominate their thoughts find that new worlds open for them. As long as enthusiasm holds out, so will new opportunities.

NORMAN VINCENT PEALE

It is a remarkable thing that some of the most optimistic and enthusiastic people you will meet are those who have been through intense suffering.

WARREN WIERSBE

God is the giver, and we are the receivers. And His richest gifts are bestowed not upon those who do the greatest things, but upon those who accept His abundance and His grace.

HANNAH WHITALL SMITH

Any time is the right time
to do with zeal
whatever pleases God.

—

ST. BASIL THE GREAT

A PRAYER FOR TODAY

Dear Lord, I know that others are watching the way that I live my life. Help me to be an enthusiastic Christian with a faith that is contagious. Amen.

YOUR THOUGHTS ABOUT ENTHUSIASM

_____

_____

_____

_____

_____

_____

_____

_____

_____

_____

_____

_____

_____

THE GIFT OF ETERNAL LIFE

*And this is the testimony: God has given us
eternal life, and this life is in His Son.
The one who has the Son has life.
The one who doesn't have the Son of God
does not have life.*

—

1 JOHN 5:11-12 HCSB

Your life here on earth is merely a preparation for a far different life to come: the eternal life that God promises to those who welcome His Son into their hearts.

As a mere mortal, your vision for the future is finite. God's vision is not burdened by such limitations: His plans extend throughout all eternity. Thus, God's plans for you are not limited to the ups and downs of everyday life. Your Heavenly Father has bigger things in mind . . . much bigger things.

How marvelous it is that God became a man and walked among us. Had He not chosen to do so, we might feel removed from a distant Creator. But ours is not a distant God. Ours is a God who understands—far better than we ever could—the essence of what it means to be human.

God understands our hopes, our fears, and our temptations. He understands what it means to be angry and what it costs to forgive. He knows the heart, the conscience, and the soul of every person who has ever lived, including you.

As you struggle with the inevitable hardships and occasional disappointments of life, remember that God has invited you to accept His abundance not only for today but also for all eternity. So keep things in perspective. Although you will inevitably encounter occasional defeats in this world, you'll have all eternity to celebrate the ultimate victory in the next.

PROMISES FROM GOD'S WORD

In a little while the world will see Me no longer, but you will see Me. Because I live, you will live too.

JOHN 14:19 HCSB

Jesus said to her, "I am the resurrection and the life. The one who believes in Me, even if he dies, will live. Everyone who lives and believes in Me will never die—ever. Do you believe this?"

JOHN 11:25-26 HCSB

Pursue righteousness, godliness, faith, love, endurance, and gentleness. Fight the good fight for the faith; take hold of eternal life, to which you were called and have made a good confession before many witnesses.

1 TIMOTHY 6:11-12 HCSB

A TIMELY TIP FROM THE GARDEN OF LOVE

People love talking about religion, and everybody has their own opinions, but ultimately only one opinion counts . . . God's. Think about God's promise of eternal life—and what that promise means to you.

MORE GREAT IDEAS

The unfolding of our friendship with the Father will be a never-ending revelation stretching on into eternity.

CATHERINE MARSHALL

God has promised us abundance, peace, and eternal life. These treasures are ours for the asking; all we must do is claim them. One of the great mysteries of life is why on earth do so many of us wait so very long to lay claim to God's gifts?

MARIE T. FREEMAN

And because we know Christ is alive, we have hope for the present and hope for life beyond the grave.

BILLY GRAHAM

Let us see the victorious Jesus, the conqueror of the tomb, the one who defied death. And let us be reminded that we, too, will be granted the same victory.

MAX LUCADO

I can still hardly believe it. I, with shriveled, bent fingers, atrophied muscles, gnarled knees, and no feeling from the shoulders down, will one day have a new body—light, bright and clothed in righteousness—powerful and dazzling.

JONI EARECKSON TADA

Your choice to either receive or reject the Lord Jesus Christ will determine where you spend eternity.

ANNE GRAHAM LOTZ

Our salvation comes to us so easily because it cost God so much.

OSWALD CHAMBERS

Life: the time God gives you to determine how you spend eternity.

ANONYMOUS

The gift of God is eternal life,
spiritual life, abundant life
through faith in Jesus Christ,
the Living Word of God.

—

ANNE GRAHAM LOTZ

A PRAYER FOR TODAY

I know, Lord, that this world is not my home; I am only here for a brief while. And, You have given me the priceless gift of eternal life through Your Son Jesus. Keep the hope of heaven fresh in my heart, and, while I am in this world, help me to pass through it with faith in my heart and praise on my lips . . . for You. Amen

⁂

YOUR THOUGHTS ABOUT
GOD'S PROMISE OF ETERNAL LIFE

_____

_____

_____

_____

_____

_____

_____

_____

_____

_____

And now abide faith, hope, love,
these three;
but the greatest of these is love.

—

1 CORINTHIANS 13:13 NKJV

MORE FROM GOD'S WORD

ANGER

A patient person [shows] great understanding, but a quick-tempered one promotes foolishness.

PROVERBS 14:29 HCSB

But now you must also put away all the following: anger, wrath, malice, slander, and filthy language from your mouth.

COLOSSIANS 3:8 HCSB

Don't let your spirit rush to be angry, for anger abides in the heart of fools.

ECCLESIASTES 7:9 HCSB

All bitterness, anger and wrath, insult and slander must be removed from you, along with all wickedness. And be kind and compassionate to one another, forgiving one another, just as God also forgave you in Christ.

EPHESIANS 4:31-32 HCSB

Everyone must be quick to hear, slow to speak, and slow to anger, for man's anger does not accomplish God's righteousness.

JAMES 1:19-20 HCSB

ATTITUDE

For the word of God is living and effective and sharper than any two-edged sword, penetrating as far as to divide soul, spirit, joints, and marrow; it is a judge of the ideas and thoughts of the heart.

HEBREWS 4:12 HCSB

Make your own attitude that of Christ Jesus.

PHILIPPIANS 2:5 HCSB

Finally brothers, whatever is true, whatever is honorable, whatever is just, whatever is pure, whatever is lovely, whatever is commendable—if there is any moral excellence and if there is any praise—dwell on these things.

PHILIPPIANS 4:8 HCSB

Set your minds on what is above, not on what is on the earth.

COLOSSIANS 3:2 HCSB

A cheerful heart has a continual feast.

PROVERBS 15:15 HCSB

CELEBRATION

This is the day the LORD has made; we will rejoice and be glad in it.

PSALM 118:24 NKJV

Rejoice in the Lord always. I will say it again: Rejoice!

PHILIPPIANS 4:4 HCSB

David and the whole house of Israel were celebrating before the Lord.

2 SAMUEL 6:5 HCSB

Their sorrow was turned into rejoicing and their mourning into a holiday. They were to be days of feasting, rejoicing, and of sending gifts to one another and the poor.

ESTHER 9:22 HCSB

At the dedication of the wall of Jerusalem, they sent for the Levites wherever they lived and brought them to Jerusalem to celebrate the joyous dedication with thanksgiving and singing accompanied by cymbals, harps, and lyres.

NEHEMIAH 12:27 HCSB

GRACE

For the law was given through Moses; grace and truth came through Jesus Christ.

JOHN 1:17 HCSB

Therefore let us approach the throne of grace with boldness, so that we may receive mercy and find grace to help us at the proper time.

HEBREWS 4:16 HCSB

Therefore, since we are receiving a kingdom that cannot be shaken, let us hold on to grace. By it, we may serve God acceptably, with reverence and awe.

HEBREWS 12:28 HCSB

For by grace you are saved through faith, and this is not from yourselves; it is God's gift—not from works, so that no one can boast.

EPHESIANS 2:8-9 HCSB

You, therefore, my child, be strong in the grace that is in Christ Jesus.

2 TIMOTHY 2:1 HCSB

HAPPINESS

How happy are those whose way is blameless, who live according to the law of the Lord! Happy are those who keep His decrees and seek Him with all their heart.

PSALM 119:1-2 HCSB

If they serve Him obediently, they will end their days in prosperity and their years in happiness.

JOB 36:11 HCSB

The one who understands a matter finds success, and the one who trusts in the Lord will be happy.

PROVERBS 16:20 HCSB

Happy are the people whose strength is in You, whose hearts are set on pilgrimage.

PSALM 84:5 HCSB

A joyful heart is good medicine, but a broken spirit dries up the bones.

PROVERBS 17:22 HCSB

LOVING GOD

He said to him, "You shall love the Lord your God with all your heart, with all your soul, and with all your mind. This is the greatest and most important commandment."

MATTHEW 22:37-38 HCSB

And we have this command from Him: the one who loves God must also love his brother.

1 JOHN 4:21 HCSB

For this is the love of God, that we keep His commandments. And His commandments are not burdensome.

1 JOHN 5:3 NKJV

Love the Lord your God with all your heart, with all your soul, and with all your strength. These words that I am giving you today are to be in your heart. Repeat them to your children. Talk about them when you sit in your house and when you walk along the road, when you lie down and when you get up.

DEUTERONOMY 6:5-7 HCSB

We love Him because He first loved us.

1 JOHN 4:19 NKJV

MATERIALISM

And He told them, "Watch out and be on guard against all greed, because one's life is not in the abundance of his possessions."

LUKE 12:15 HCSB

For what does it benefit a man to gain the whole world yet lose his life? What can a man give in exchange for his life?

MARK 8:36-37 HCSB

Don't collect for yourselves treasures on earth, where moth and rust destroy and where thieves break in and steal. But collect for yourselves treasures in heaven, where neither moth nor rust destroys, and where thieves don't break in and steal. For where your treasure is, there your heart will be also.

MATTHEW 6:19-21 HCSB

For the mind-set of the flesh is death, but the mind-set of the Spirit is life and peace.

ROMANS 8:6 HCSB

OBEDIENCE

Therefore, get your minds ready for action, being self-disciplined, and set your hope completely on the grace to be brought to you at the revelation of Jesus Christ. As obedient children, do not be conformed to the desires of your former ignorance but, as the One who called you is holy, you also are to be holy in all your conduct.

1 PETER 1:13-15 HCSB

And the world with its lust is passing away, but the one who does God's will remains forever.

1 JOHN 2:17 HCSB

Now by this we know that we know Him, if we keep His commandments. . . . But whoever keeps His word, truly the love of God is perfected in him. By this we know that we are in Him. He who says he abides in Him ought himself also to walk just as He walked.

1 JOHN 2:3, 5-6 NKJV

For this is what love for God is: to keep His commands. Now His commands are not a burden, because whatever has been born of God conquers the world. This is the victory that has conquered the world: our faith.

1 JOHN 5:3-4 HCSB

PRIDE

Your eyes are set against the proud—You humble them.

2 SAMUEL 22:28 HCSB

Do not love the world or the things that belong to the world. If anyone loves the world, love for the Father is not in him. Because everything that belongs to the world—the lust of the flesh, the lust of the eyes, and the pride in one's lifestyle—is not from the Father, but is from the world.

1 JOHN 2:15-16 HCSB

But as for me, I will never boast about anything except the cross of our Lord Jesus Christ, through whom the world has been crucified to me, and I to the world.

GALATIANS 6:14 HCSB

The arrogant will stumble and fall with no one to pick him up.

JEREMIAH 50:32 HCSB

Do nothing out of rivalry or conceit, but in humility consider others as more important than yourselves.

PHILIPPIANS 2:3 HCSB

PROBLEMS

Your heart must not be troubled. Believe in God; believe also in Me.

JOHN 14:1 HCSB

God is our refuge and strength, a very present help in trouble.

PSALM 46:1 NKJV

I will be with you when you pass through the waters . . . when you walk through the fire . . . the flame will not burn you. For I the Lord your God, the Holy One of Israel, and your Savior.

ISAIAH 43:2-3 HCSB

The righteous is rescued from trouble; in his place, the wicked goes in.

PROVERBS 11:8 HCSB

Then they cried out to the Lord in their trouble, and He saved them out of their distresses.

PSALM 107:13 NKJV

RIGHTEOUSNESS

Because the eyes of the Lord are on the righteous and His ears are open to their request. But the face of the Lord is against those who do evil.

1 PETER 3:12 HCSB

Therefore, come out from among them and be separate, says the Lord; do not touch any unclean thing, and I will welcome you.

2 CORINTHIANS 6:17 HCSB

Flee from youthful passions, and pursue righteousness, faith, love, and peace, along with those who call on the Lord from a pure heart.

2 TIMOTHY 2:22 HCSB

And now, Israel, what does the Lord your God ask of you except to fear the Lord your God by walking in all His ways, to love Him, and to worship the Lord your God with all your heart and all your soul?

DEUTERONOMY 10:12 HCSB

STRESS

Cast your burden on the Lord, and He shall sustain you; He shall never permit the righteous to be moved.

PSALM 55:22 NKJV

Your heart must not be troubled. Believe in God; believe also in Me.

JOHN 14:1 HCSB

Then they cried out to the Lord in their trouble, and He saved them out of their distresses.

PSALM 107:13 NKJV

For You, O God, have tested us; You have refined us as silver is refined. You brought us into the net; You laid affliction on our backs. You have caused men to ride over our heads; we went through fire and through water; but You brought us out to rich fulfillment.

PSALM 66:10–12 NKJV

Rejoice in hope; be patient in affliction; be persistent in prayer.

ROMANS 12:12 HCSB

233

TALENTS

Do not neglect the gift that is in you.

1 TIMOTHY 4:14 HCSB

Each one has his own gift from God, one in this manner and another in that.

1 CORINTHIANS 7:7 NKJV

So he who had received five talents came and brought five other talents, saying, "Lord, you delivered to me five talents; look, I have gained five more talents besides them." His lord said to him, "Well done, good and faithful servant; you were faithful over a few things, I will make you ruler over many things. Enter into the joy of your lord."

MATTHEW 25:20-21 NKJV

I remind you to keep ablaze the gift of God that is in you.

2 TIMOTHY 1:6 HCSB

Based on the gift they have received, everyone should use it to serve others, as good managers of the varied grace of God.

1 PETER 4:10 HCSB

TEACHING

Set an example of good works yourself, with integrity and dignity in your teaching.

TITUS 2:7 HCSB

Teach a youth about the way he should go; even when he is old he will not depart from it.

PROVERBS 22:6 HCSB

According to the grace given to us, we have different gifts: If prophecy, use it according to the standard of faith; if service, in service; if teaching, in teaching; if exhorting, in exhortation; giving, with generosity; leading, with diligence; showing mercy, with cheerfulness.

ROMANS 12:6-8 HCSB

Be conscientious about yourself and your teaching; persevere in these things, for by doing this you will save both yourself and your hearers.

1 TIMOTHY 4:13 HCSB

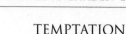

TEMPTATION

No temptation has overtaken you except what is common to humanity. God is faithful and He will not allow you to be tempted beyond what you are able, but with the temptation He will also provide a way of escape, so that you are able to bear it.

1 CORINTHIANS 10:13 HCSB

Do not be deceived: "Bad company corrupts good morals."

1 CORINTHIANS 15:33 HCSB

Be sober! Be on the alert! Your adversary the Devil is prowling around like a roaring lion, looking for anyone he can devour.

1 PETER 5:8 HCSB

The Lord knows how to deliver the godly out of temptations.

2 PETER 2:9 NKJV

Put on the full armor of God so that you can stand against the tactics of the Devil.

EPHESIANS 6:11 HCSB

YOUR TESTIMONY

But sanctify the Lord God in your hearts, and always be ready to give a defense to everyone who asks you a reason for the hope that is in you.

1 PETER 3:15 HCSB

You are the light of the world. A city that is set on a hill cannot be hidden. Nor do they light a lamp and put it under a basket, but on a lampstand, and it gives light to all who are in the house. Let your light so shine before men, that they may see your good works and glorify your Father in heaven.

MATTHEW 5:14–16 NKJV

Whatever I tell you in the dark, speak in the light; and what you hear in the ear, preach on the housetops.

MATTHEW 10:27 NKJV

And I say to you, anyone who acknowledges Me before men, the Son of Man will also acknowledge him before the angels of God; but whoever denies Me before men will be denied before the angels of God.

LUKE 12:8-9 HCSB

TRUTH

For everyone who practices wicked things hates the light and avoids it, so that his deeds may not be exposed. But anyone who lives by the truth comes to the light, so that his works may be shown to be accomplished by God.

JOHN 3:20–21 HCSB

Be diligent to present yourself approved to God, a worker who doesn't need to be ashamed, correctly teaching the word of truth.

2 TIMOTHY 2:15 HCSB

I have no greater joy than this: to hear that my children are walking in the truth.

3 JOHN 1:4 HCSB

You have already heard about this hope in the message of truth, the gospel that has come to you. It is bearing fruit and growing all over the world, just as it has among you since the day you heard it and recognized God's grace in the truth.

COLOSSIANS 1:5-6 HCSB

WISDOM

Therefore, everyone who hears these words of Mine and acts on them will be like a sensible man who built his house on the rock. The rain fell, the rivers rose, and the winds blew and pounded that house. Yet it didn't collapse, because its foundation was on the rock.

MATTHEW 7:24–25 HCSB

But from Him you are in Christ Jesus, who for us became wisdom from God, as well as righteousness, sanctification, and redemption.

1 CORINTHIANS 1:30 HCSB

For God has not given us a spirit of fearfulness, but one of power, love, and sound judgment.

2 TIMOTHY 1:7 HCSB

Now if any of you lacks wisdom, he should ask God, who gives to all generously and without criticizing, and it will be given to him.

JAMES 1:5 HCSB

WORLDLINESS

Pure and undefiled religion before our God and Father is this: to look after orphans and widows in their distress and to keep oneself unstained by the world.

JAMES 1:27 HCSB

Now we have not received the spirit of the world, but the Spirit who is from God, in order to know what has been freely given to us by God.

1 CORINTHIANS 2:12 HCSB

No one should deceive himself. If anyone among you thinks he is wise in this age, he must become foolish so that he can become wise. For the wisdom of this world is foolishness with God, since it is written: He catches the wise in their craftiness.

1 CORINTHIANS 3:18-19 HCSB

Do not love the world or the things that belong to the world. If anyone loves the world, love for the Father is not in him.

1 JOHN 2:15 HCSB

Do not have other gods besides Me.

EXODUS 20:3 HCSB